JE   '10

W9-BBD-213

Good, Better, Best

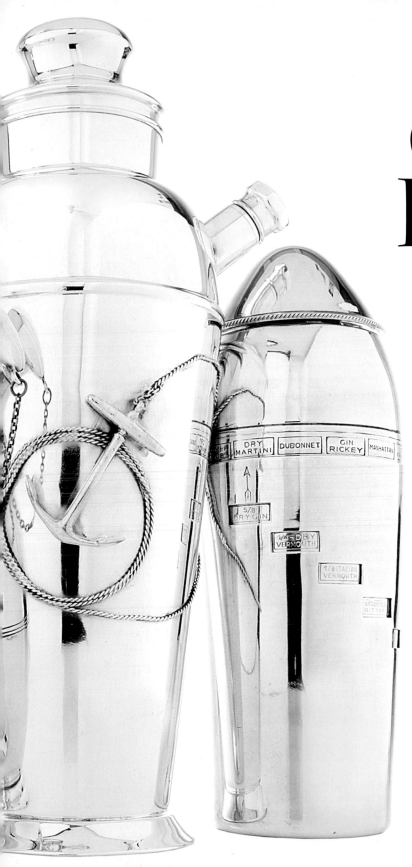

Good, Better, Best

Trade Secrets for Spotting a "Find"

✳

Carol Prisant

Mount Laurel Library
100 Walt Whitman Avenue
Mount Laurel, NJ 08054-9539
856-234-7319
www.mtlaurel.lib.nj.us

WITHDRAWN

Viking Studio

VIKING STUDIO
Published by the Penguin Group
Penguin Group (USA) Inc., 375 Hudson Street,
New York, New York 10014, U.S.A.
Penguin Group (Canada), 90 Eglinton Avenue East, Suite 700,
Toronto, Ontario, Canada M4P 2Y3
(a division of Pearson Penguin Canada Inc.)
Penguin Books Ltd, 80 Strand, London WC2R 0RL, England
Penguin Ireland, 25 St. Stephen's Green, Dublin 2, Ireland
(a division of Penguin Books Ltd)
Penguin Books Australia Ltd, 250 Camberwell Road, Camberwell,
Victoria 3124, Australia
(a division of Pearson Australia Group Pty Ltd)
Penguin Books India Pvt Ltd, 11 Community Centre, Panchsheel Park,
New Delhi – 110 017, India
Penguin Group (NZ), 67 Apollo Drive, Rosedale, North Shore 0632,
New Zealand (a division of Pearson New Zealand Ltd)
Penguin Books (South Africa) (Pty) Ltd, 24 Sturdee Avenue,
Rosebank, Johannesburg 2196, South Africa

Penguin Books Ltd, Registered Offices:
80 Strand, London WC2R 0RL, England

First published in 2009 by Viking Studio,
a member of Penguin Group (USA) Inc.

1 3 5 7 9 10 8 6 4 2
Copyright © Carol Prisant, 2009
All rights reserved

Portions of this book first appeared in different form in issues of *House Beautiful*.

Illustration credits appear on pages 137–140.

ISBN 978-0-14-200527-9

Printed in Malaysia
Set in Hoefler Titling and Clarendon Light
Designed by Linda Kocur

Without limiting the rights under copyright reserved above, no part of this publication may be
reproduced, stored in or introduced into a retrieval system, or transmitted, in any form or by any means
(electronic, mechanical, photocopying, recording or otherwise), without the prior written permission
of both the copyright owner and the above publisher of this book.

The scanning, uploading, and distribution of this book via the Internet or via any other means without the
permission of the publisher is illegal and punishable by law. Please purchase only authorized
electronic editions and do not participate in or encourage electronic piracy of copyrightable materials.
Your support of the author's rights is appreciated.

While the author has made every effort to provide accurate telephone numbers and Internet addresses
at the time of publication, neither the publisher nor the author assumes any responsibility for errors,
or for changes that occur after publication.
Further, publisher does not have any control over and does not assume any responsibility
for author or third-party Web sites or their content.

To Barden
and
Sandy
and
always, Millard

Contents

Introduction

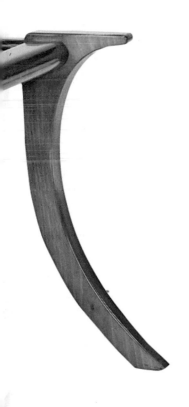

When I went into the antiques business in 1965, the world seemed to be full of people who wouldn't buy from me because I looked too young to know much about antiques. In their defense, antiques were then very serious things, very intimidating, and had to have been made before 1832 (the start of Queen Victoria's reign). I felt it was a real disadvantage not to have gray hair and perhaps a nice shawl to help me sell my stock convincingly. The shawl would have been easy enough to get, but sad to say, I wasn't really selling anything that required credibility. I was peddling flowery cups and saucers, Frenchy lamps, a toy bulldog, a footstool, and an empty frame or two because those were the things I'd bought with the $200 my mother had given me to "go into the antiques business." (It took me three months to spend that

$200.) My mother thought, charitably, that I'd be good at antiques because I'd furnished my first apartment with bargains like a $12 brass bed, a rice paper painting of butterflies for $3, a decent desk for only $50, and once, a pair of painfully expensive $35 vases. (I still have them all.) But in fact, I was shopping at antiques stores because (a) the things in department stores were too expensive for my husband's and my tiny budget and (b) the things in other stores at the time were Scandinavian and teak and amoeba-shaped and far too modern for me. Silly kid. Who knew that all that plastic, plywood, and walnut would grow up to be today's museum-worthy Midcentury Modern. Instead, I took that start-up money and bought mid- and low-level pretties, exhibiting initially in down-and-dirty antiques shows (the first of the Twenty-sixth Street flea markets, among others), then in glossier antiques shows (at Madison Square Garden and the New York

armories), and finally, in my own Long Island store. Along the way, I read up on my subject like mad. Unfortunately, most antiques books at that time dealt with major, major treasures, which is how I learned more than I would ever need to know about eighteenth-century French furniture, early pewter, and Sèvres porcelain, instead of what I was more likely to see, and indeed saw: the pretty ordinary stuff with which nineteenth-century Americans furnished their homes, namely needlepoint pictures, unresearchable Chinese carvings, wax portraits, and lots of what would later become known as Folk Art. Whenever I bought something I couldn't identify—and there was a lot of that at first—there were only those grandiose books for guidance. My fellow dealers, whom I asked for help, were either as ignorant as I was or, if they had a little knowledge, wouldn't have considered sharing it with a competitor. Because there were no schools to teach my subject, I read. But even when I finally found a reference or a picture of the mystery I'd found in that last freezing attic, there were no price guides or online references or auction results around It was every entrepreneurial housewife for herself.

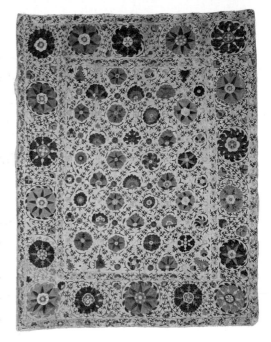

It turned out, though, that the majority of my fellow dealers, especially those in the New York suburbs, didn't read much at all. So as my own library expanded over the years to include books on paper-weights, silhouettes, Windsor chairs, art glass, and every other type of object that I was sure I'd just sold for too little, I was eventually able to buy from other shops the scores of "finds" that helped my business thrive. How did I know what to sell them for? I added on a fair profit, and learned, the hard way, to allow for bargaining. If a thing sold too fast, I'd made a mistake, and I bought a book. If it didn't sell at all, I marked it down until it did, and bought a book. My business model was seat of the pants. And when other dealers bought from me—which they did because the antiques business really exists because dealers buy from

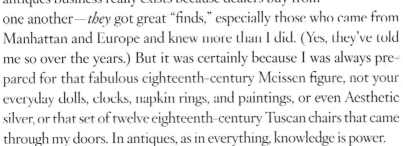

one another—*they* got great "finds," especially those who came from Manhattan and Europe and knew more than I did. (Yes, they've told me so over the years.) But it was certainly because I was always prepared for that fabulous eighteenth-century Meissen figure, not your everyday dolls, clocks, napkin rings, and paintings, or even Aesthetic silver, or that set of twelve eighteenth-century Tuscan chairs that came through my doors. In antiques, as in everything, knowledge is power.

Forty years in the business have taught me a few things I couldn't learn in books: That an object can be ugly as sin but still worth a fortune. That a thing can be complex, gilded, and gorgeous and still be relatively worthless. That there's Damage, and there's damage. That a nicked and scratched piece of glass is relegated to cabinet-piece status, while a nicked and scratched piece of furniture merely has patina. That despite the primacy of Midcentury Modern (the latest version of the paradigm shift that regularly occurs when dealers run out of previously overlooked—that is, cheap—things to buy), there are millions who still love old-fashioned stuff. That antiques are getting younger every year and, in all likelihood, will be catching up with us next week. Don't look back. They're absolutely gaining on us.

This book is the one I didn't have: a picture book with concise explanations for people who care that they're getting value for money.

People who'd love to own antiques or vintage objects, but who are afraid they don't know enough to go out and buy. People who've inherited a "something" that looks like the something they saw on *Antiques Roadshow,* but aren't sure if it's really authentic or some old reproduction. People who've listened to an antiques dealer's sales pitch and known that there was one right question to ask, but didn't know what it was. People who've won an item in an Internet auction and discovered that Chippendale "style" doesn't mean Chippendale era. In short, people who aren't so knowledgeable and self-confident that they've never had to hide an embarrassing mistake in the basement— or even worse, burn it.

Have you ever considered spending so much for something old that you've had to think three times about it, and wished that you could make a quick phone call to someone like me? I'd be happy to talk to you if you called, and even look at your cell phone snapshot, but half an hour later the two of us would still be on the phone while I told you exactly what bits to look at, feel, and smell (yes, sometimes smell),

before you buy. By that time, of course, someone else will have snatched your prize from under your nose. Or the tag sale will be over. Or the dealer will be closing up shop and you won't be up in Maine for another year. And that's why you need a good do-it-yourself book: a kind of you-can-be-your-own appraiser book. A book to tuck in your car or your pocket to reach for when you really need help. A book so useful that, eventually, there'll be little in furniture, glass, porcelain, jewelry, or art that you won't be able to intelligently assess by yourself. I can't promise that you'll always buy the "best," but if you do buy the "good," it will only be because you love it.

The trick—if it can be called a trick—is in knowing exactly what to look at. When I owned my shop, people would sometimes bring in a vase or a chair for me to evaluate together with a book or magazine article in which would be pictured a fabulously expensive and rare vase or chair "just like" the one they proudly displayed. What they didn't see—because there is *so* much to know— as that the "identical" vase in the book was signed, while their example wasn't; that its particular signature was rarer than the first Beatles record, while their unsigned vase was one of thousands. And the chair pictured in the book? It was usually the work of a master carver or cabinetmaker whose furniture was in museums, while the chair they'd hauled in to show to me was usually made 150 years later by a copyist who couldn't carve a holiday turkey. What they needed to know was that proportions can be wrong. Feet can be wrong. Woods can be thin veneers. Diamonds can be zircons. Gold paint is not gold leaf. Paintings can be overcleaned. Porcelain can be inconspicuously mended. It's a jungle out there. And I haven't even touched on fakes, forgeries, and the honest homage.

In my years of traveling and braking for "Antiques" signs (and sometimes, embarrassingly, just "Tiques" signs), I've noticed something interesting: The farther I traveled from big cities, the more expensive the antiques became. Which made me wonder why it was that a piece of workaday Victorian furniture could be priced higher in rural Georgia than in St. Louis, for instance; or why the identical Tiffany & Co. mug from the 1970s should be selling for twice as much in Austin as in New York. Or why, in East Liverpool, anything gilded was generally more costly than anything plain. The answer turned out to be that these objects were actually rarities in those towns. The shop owners, so far away from urban centers, had never seen enough good Victorian furniture or enough Tiffany silver to be able to judge *relative* quality. They didn't know

how unusual or rare a seventies Tiffany silver mug might be because, having only seen one—this one—they were dazzled by that Tiffany name and overpriced it. The smart antiquer (and the smart dealer) has to know a lot about relativity. She or he has to know that this sunburst mirror, for instance, is worth more, or maybe very much more, than that look-alike mirror. Ergo, *Good, Better, Best.* Prices will go up or down with the passage of time, of course, but the relative value of the "good" painting, for example, to the "better" painting or the "best" painting will *never, ever* change. And that's why, if you've absorbed the explanations, encouragements, and warnings in the pages that follow, you'll have a really decent handle on things that experienced professionals take years to learn. You will know how to tell the difference between the good, the better, and the best. And if you wind up buying the best piece for the money you have to spend, I'll have done my job.

There are, of course, millions of antiques out there, and probably a million types of antiques too, if you take into account all the kinds of furniture, porcelain, glass, clocks, lamps, paintings, jewelry, prints, and sculptures that have been created over the centuries. And that's not even including another million or so vintage things, such as plywood furniture, Depression glass, Art Deco clocks, lava lamps, Line Vautrin mirrors, Folk Art quilts, and PEZ dispensers. (And by the way, those are just European and American examples.) How is it possible to choose among them all? Well, not coincidentally, a majority of the "helpful hints" in this book are based mainly on American objects and lean heavily toward the generic. For example, I might tell you that you don't want to buy a refinished Queen Anne cabinet, but this rule is also true for Shaker cabinets and Eames cabinets. (You knew that, of course.) But did you know that a Staffordshire platter depicting hounds attacking a wild boar has a good deal in common with a Gainsborough portrait of an old woman? Both are "difficult" subjects, and both, with the exception of works by such icons as Rembrandt or Van Gogh, are considerably less valuable than other paintings or platters. There are hundreds of such correspondencies, though, and I've tried to arrange things so that they occur across and within all the categories in this book. (Which means you'll become very familiar with some types of advice!) So that's why I've selected only objects that I think are terrific learning tools: those that illustrate or represent the really useful nuggets of information.

Before we begin our mining operations, however, let's take a minute out for fakes. Everyone wants to know about fakes and how to spot them. And of course, there are excellent fakes these days, for with the abundance of convincing synthetic materials and laser-cutting technology, they're improving year by year. Yet there's a simple piece of information that will save you frantic searches and sleepless nights:

Scammers don't fake things that aren't really, *really* valuable. Why, after all, would they waste their time and talents on ordinary stuff? Or more to the point, on anything for which there isn't a substantial moneyed market? That's why, unless you're an "advanced" collector (and if you are, you certainly don't need this book), you're unlikely to be buying things that might be fakes.

I take that back. It's true in just about every field but painting. Paintings have been reproduced since they were first created, sometimes even by the artist who painted them, who often made one or more "reproductions." Until the era of photography, that was the only way to show or sell a work with a popular subject. A reproduction is not a fake, because a fake is intended to deceive. European travelers of the nineteenth century often brought home copies of great works, canvases that were frequently the work of art students (or starving artists). Nobody was "faking" anything. Unless, that is, the imitation was such a good one that the "signature" of the original artist could be added to it later. But because of that possibility, paintings that are murkily dark and old (including those signed Monet or Corot) can be suspect. If you own one of these, or are merely thinking of buying one and spending an uncomfortable amount of money on the purchase, call in an expert appraiser before you buy. These days it's easy, because a photo of the front and back can be e-mailed to the right expert anywhere in the world for an opinion. Where do you find this expert? Would it surprise you to know that the prices paid, the owners' names, and even the sale dates of the majority of paintings—even unimportant paintings—by first- and second-tier artists have been recorded for decades in catalogues raisonnés? The authors of these catalogues are often still alive, and happy to see and vet a possible work by "their" artist. Paintings are among the most expensive of collectible treasures, and they require the most research.

A Few Things to Consider When You're Looking at Antiques

Color Vibrant color is what you want in an antique. Or at least the color the piece was born with. For example, a hand-colored print that's been hung in the sun will fade, which is why, if you're looking at three versions of the same Currier and Ives bowl of fruit, the one that's brightest is the one to buy. Don't have three at once? Check the books or go online to see those that are in museums. (Keep in mind that color can be "refreshed," which diminishes value.)

Color can help you in establishing a date too. If you know that the Chinese didn't discover a certain shade of blue until 1800, for instance, you won't buy that Mingish vase.

Condition Here's a basic rule: The older a thing is, the more forgiving collectors are prepared to be about its condition. This means that a fifteenth-century Venetian glass compote can be cracked and repaired, and retain its value, but a Louis Comfort Tiffany glass compote from the turn of the twentieth century won't. There are more of the latter around, and rarity equals value. To take things one step further, when objects are even more recent and have been mass-produced—for example, toy robots, aluminum trays, Fiesta Dinnerware—perfection (sometimes known as mint in box) is expected.

Function Watches and lamps have a function. Paintings and snuffboxes don't. Some people prefer to collect things with a function, but if you've ever marveled at the price of a sampler or a jade carving, it will be obvious to you that some people couldn't care less. Antique and vintage objects don't have to be functional to be valuable. Nevertheless, if a thing *does* have a function, like a clock, music box, or Donald Duck nodder, collectors prefer it to be working, just as they prefer tables to have the requisite number of legs.

Market Value There is a legal definition of market value: It's the price agreed upon by a willing buyer and a willing seller. There are other types of value, of course—historical value, celebrity value, intrinsic value—but market value is the value of a piece in the current marketplace, and that's what I've chosen to use for this book. Prices may fluctuate over time, it's true—doorstops may become less collectible, posters of the Rolling Stones may not be cherished by generations that have never heard of them—but auction results remain the standard of market value for appraisers and collectors.

They're unquestionably the very public price agreed upon by a willing buyer and a willing seller.

One of the most curious and valuable side effects of eBay has been that a collector from Scottsdale, say, who once believed she owned the only Vucko Wolf PEZ Dispenser around, now knows that hers is merely one of thousands. It's been painful but instructive to find that eBay is not just a market barometer, but also a market leveler. And it's tops for comparison shopping, though the drawback is that you may not find on eBay the *exact* doll you're agonizing about this week in your local trash-'n'-treasure store. You may remember that it appeared on eBay within this last month, but it may have disappeared—been bought or withdrawn—just when you need it for comparison. That's why it's a good thing to own a book you can refer to when you shop, so you'll feel secure in buying (or passing up) that coffee table, lamp, or doll.

Materials Materials can reveal the true age of an object. You're not likely to find chrome trim, to take an obvious example, on a French desk from 1780. (Actually, you're not likely to find a French desk from 1780, but for argument's sake, let's say you might.) You won't expect to find our hypothetical desk veneered in walnut, either. Walnut may have been popular in England's Queen Anne era, but the last Louis loved fruitwood veneers. Your desk isn't likely to be solid (that is, unveneered) mahogany either, because mahogany was never as fashionable in France as it was in England, Ireland, and America, quite probably because it wasn't an easy import.

Consider platinum too, which wasn't in use in nineteenth-century jewelry. If you're looking at a platinum wristwatch, you can be certain it was made in the twentieth century. A quick check of Wikipedia or an encyclopedia for the chronology and availability of a particular material—metal, wood, textile dyes, lacquer—might spare you decades of buyer's remorse.

Ornamentation Ornamentation is like icing on a cake: By itself, it adds nothing but "more." What's important about ornamentation is how well it's done. Furniture can have a lot or a little, and so can glass, porcelain, silver, gold, bronze, and so on. Hand painting on a plate is ornamentation, but slapdash painting can spoil that plate, just as crude carving will ruin an otherwise handsome table (not to mention excessive gilding, which has been known to make people ill). So you need to ask yourself about any ornamented piece, does its "icing" enhance its beauty? After that, it's just a matter of your taste and your checkbook.

Provenance There are only a few items in this book with a provenance—a history of ownership, a pedigree. You may own a silver teapot that belonged to your great-grandmother, and without a doubt that teapot has a legitimate provenance. But unless your great-grandmother was Eleanor Roosevelt, its provenance wouldn't make a bit of difference to its fair market value. On the other hand, if you have a run-of-the-mill table that once belonged to Princess Margaret (and the documents to prove it), well . . . . (see page 99).

Regional Value I've mentioned that in various parts of this country you might see a selection of prices for the very same item. But certain types of antiques and vintage objects are also valuable only in their own part of the country. San Francisco silver, for example, is much sought after by California museums, so if you own some and want to sell it, sell it there, but don't expect to find a big audience for it in New York. Western items are bigger out west than in Rhode Island, and California and Florida painters bring a good deal more in their home states than anywhere else. This is regional value. We are all chauvinists at heart.

Style In the antiques and vintage world, style is a familiar word. You have Victorian style, Midcentury Modern style, Art Deco style, and so on, and each comprises a distinctive group of designs that appear in many of the objects made in one particular era. Each, too, has its fans.

But there is another use of "style," and it's an important one. When a seller (auction gallery, shop, or Internet merchant) describes a piece as "Tiffany style" or "Sheraton style," that's a red flag to the collector, because it's accepted practice in the antiques world that the term "style" describes anything that's *not* of the period. In other words, "Roman style" or "Art Nouveau style" (unless the seller isn't a professional and doesn't know better) indicates a reproduction.

These days, I have gray hair at last, and with it, some credibility. Unexpectedly, I still don't have as much knowledge as I'd like, and am almost resigned to the likelihood that I never will. The more I learn, I've found, the more there is to learn. I'm still surprised, for instance, by things I see on *Antiques Roadshow.* (I would *never* have spotted that Indian blanket!) Nevertheless, I think it's time to pass along something of my experience. I can't pretend to offer you everything there is to know, but I can give you a better start than I had. If I'd only known then what I know now! (And had that $200 to spend again.)

Good, Better, Best

Nineteenth-Century Enameled Glass

The painting is of good quality and the gilding is in fine condition, which accounts for its selling price of $700.

Large pieces of glass are often more valuable, although this almost 16-inch vase was probably one of a pair meant for a mantel.

Check the bottom for a signature, which may be etched or cut into the glass right on the rim, and hard to see. (Vase painters, however, were often women, who wouldn't have signed their work.) This vase, as is usual with French opaline, has none.

A Little Backstory

Enameled and painted glass resemble each other, but they're not alike. Yes, both are done with a brush, but the "paint" on enameled glass is actually a combination of colored glass powders, metallic oxides, and oil, and after the decoration is complete, the glass is reheated and the enamels bond to the surface. Paint is just paint. It flakes and fades. Because their embellishment makes both types more fragile than other types of glass, they're happiest in a cabinet.

Q & A

When was this sort of glass popular?
The extensive use of flora and fauna as decoration is a Victorian giveaway. These pieces are almost always late Victorian (the queen reigned from 1837–1901), and to our modern eyes, are always a little fussy.

But this is all hand painted, isn't it? Shouldn't that make it very expensive?
You'd think so, but these days, painstaking technique has little to do with desirability. So while it would cost quite a bit for us to reproduce even a good example, current fashions in design and the art world affect what people want to collect. Nevertheless, there are Moser collectors, just as there are collectors for the work of the Victorian artist William-Adolphe Bouguereau.

Do you think interest in this glass will ever revive?
The craze for art glass in the 1960s and 1970s carried some of these Victorian painted pieces along with it. There's little interest in Victoriana these days, but it may revive (given my eighty year-cycle theory) in 2040 . . . or so.

I suppose one shouldn't put it in the dishwasher?
Not a good idea, although people do, usually because they don't know any better. Nineteenth- and some twentieth-century paints won't tolerate dishwasher detergents. They'll be gone in a flash.

Look For

- Enameled, rather than painted glass
- Signed glass (check on the bottom or within the design)
- Brilliant-colored paints, an indication of nineteenth-century manufacture
- Birds and flowers—more popular than stags
- Several combined techniques, that is, gilding, enameling, applied glass decoration

Stay Away From

- Worn gilding, usually on the rims and feet
- Missing bits of applied glass beads or drops—such "jewels" were often used in conjunction with the painted enamels
- Chips in the paint
- The usual cracks, chips, or evidences of repair to the glass
- Glass with worn or faded paint

Good It looked like it might be Moser glass to the seller, but this very tall (17-inch) enamel decorated glass vase didn't convince the buyers in the audience on the day of the sale. It sold for only $88.00.

Better Fanciful and exuberant, this enamel-decorated ruffled bride's basket was often used for candy or flowers, and was a fixture on dining room tables toward the end of the nineteenth century. The bowl is often genuine art glass, made by Mt. Washington, or one of the other American manufacturers. But this is not one of those. Its seller termed it art glass, nevertheless, perhaps because of the shaded pink interior. It brought $470, which is about right, maybe a little high.

Best Also large, like the "good" example, this enameled, gilt, and applied glass green-tinted vase *is* by the famous Moser factory. It was estimated to bring $4,000 to $6,000, but sold for $3,200, maybe because of its condition—the beautifully rendered bird of prey in the center has lost its glass eye, and there are chips in the branch.

Midcentury Dining Chairs

The style of the chairs needn't match the style of your table unless you're doing a fifties dining room.

Materials should reflect the age of the chairs. Teak and brass are just what you want to see in Finn Juhl's chairs from 1953.

Flip a chair over and check for a label (or in this case, a branded manufacturer's mark: *Bovirke Copenhagen—Made in Denmark*) under the seat.

A Little Backstory

Chairs are favorites with both designers and collectors, possibly because the individual chair can be highly sculptural. Sets of chairs, however, ought to be truly functional. After all, they're yanked out and pushed under tables; subjected to spilled wine and sticky fingers; and sat in, on all too many occasions over the years, by diners far heavier than had ever been anticipated by their designers. Midcentury Modern chairs can take all of the above, and they're innovative besides.

Q & A

How many chairs actually constitute a set of dining room chairs?
For Midcentury Modern, that number would depend
on the size of the original table for which the set was
purchased. A buyer might order eight side chairs, or six
side chairs and two arm chairs, or twelve chairs. There is no
such thing as a standard number for sets of chairs.

Is the upholstery important?
Collectors love to see original upholstery, particularly if it's
in a popular pattern or material of the period in which the
chair was made, and in especially good condition. Leather
seems to hold up best, and well-worn leather—not cracked
or dried out—is very attractive to buyers of Midcentury
Modern furniture.

*But maybe the fabric has been reupholstered. How do I know if the
upholstery and the frame were "born together"?*
If they've been recovered and the frame is wood, there
should be extra sets of holes under the seat. (Peel one edge
of the fabric back a bit to look.) If a few chairs of a set
have been recovered, you'll see differing types of wear and
changes in coloration.

*How do I know if the ten chairs in my set were all purchased
together?*
Many sets of chairs were made to order and individually
numbered by their manufacturers. Sometimes, that
fat diner comes along, though, and one chair has to be
replaced. That's how your set of ten comes to be missing
the chair numbered 4. Sometimes owners decide to order
another four chairs as their family grows. And sometimes
dealers "assemble" a set. In other words, the table they
bought came with five chairs, and they've picked up three
more matching singles.

Look For

- Original upholstery
- Numbered chairs
- Labels (as usual)
- Iconic shapes from the decade that interests you

Stay Away From

- Broken backs
- Broken legs
- Boring designs—there is still enough of this furniture on the
  market that you ought to be able to find a set that is interesting.
- Assembled sets (see above)

Good Björn Winblad is better known for whimsical porcelain
than for furniture. This fairly groovy set of eight chairs, circa 1975,
is made of lacquered wood with printed and lacquered acrylic.
Signed and numbered on the backrest, they sold for $8,400.

Better A mere four of these "Chippendale" chairs in Robert
Venturi's tongue-in-cheek Grandmother pattern sold for $10,200,
almost twice the price of the eight "good" chairs above. Made of
plywood, plastic laminate, and rubber, they were retailed by the
United States firm Knoll in 1984.

Best Since 1961, these six Danish chairs by Poul Kjaerholm
have been in the possession of one family. Signed and impressed
on the underside with the manufacturer's mark and upholstered in
their original leather, the six brought $66,000.

Many oriental rugs of the same type are more or less the same sizes because of the sizing of local looms. This early twentieth-century Heriz, at almost 18 feet by 11 feet 2 inches is somewhat larger than usual.

It's missing the end guard borders (compare the ends to the sides).

It's an ideal room size, and brought $13,200.

Folding for storage can leave permanent marks. This rug has suffered foldwear (not visible in this image). Minor repairs are acceptable. Parts of this rug have been repiled and there is minor retinting of the colors.

A Little Backstory

Handmade oriental rugs, usually woven of wool pile on a cotton warp (that's the vertical thread) are traditionally named for the villages or towns in which they are made. Most rugs (except for prayer rugs) can be used in either direction, and many old and good rugs have withstood dogs, vacuuming, red wine, and moths to be handed down to us in surprisingly fine condition. They're tough and beautiful, which accounts for their perennial popularity.

Good A popular size, this 9 ½ × 12-foot Heriz has a brick-color center medallion and the blazingly strong hues that usually indicate a rug of modern manufacture. This twentieth-century example brought $3,700.

Better A rug has to be one hundred or more years old to be an antique. An antique Heriz is a Serapi. This well-preserved 1890 Serapi, approximately 9 × 12 feet, sold for $7,500.

Best Almost 10 × 12 feet, and handmade, this softly faded Serapi seems both subtle and bold. This rather primitive carpet is everything the "good" carpet would like to be. It brought $22,230.

Look For

- Silk carpets, which feel soft and slippery
- Fringes at two ends (see below)
- Small knots and fine weaving—count the knots per inch; the more, the better
- Very early carpets
- Abrash, a band of distinct color change, which marks the old, handmade carpet
- Evenly worn pile
- Design that appears on both the front and the back of a carpet indicates a piece is handmade.
- Careful repairs, which are acceptable

Stay Away From

- Extensively repainted carpets—you can't see the wear
- Abrash intentionally woven into brand-new carpets
- Dry and crisp wool or silk carpets
- Missing fringes (all rugs once ended in fringes, the ends of the warp)
- Chemically washed rugs from the 1920s—this softened the colors, but also damaged the fibers
- Serious dog stains

Q & A

Oriental rugs all look so much alike. Are some designs or types better than others?
Fashions in rugs change, just as they do in the other decorative arts. Last year, maybe everyone wanted Persian rugs, but this year, it's all about Caucasians. It's always better to choose a rug that pleases your own eye. You can sometimes find bargains that way.

But there are colors that are more desirable, aren't there?
Rugs with a considerable amount of green in them seem to be uncommon and are therefore sought after. But do be wary of color. On old carpets that are worn, colors—all colors—have often been repainted. Wet a cloth and rub the surface to determine if a rug has had a recent touch-up, called tinting.

I've heard other buyers talking about knot size. What does that mean?
Each stitch in a rug is actually a knot, and generally speaking, the smaller the size of the knot (look at the back of the rug), the finer the workmanship and the finer the design. Persian carpets, often made in cities rather than by nomads or village weavers, frequently have curved and floral designs and these can be as beautiful to look at on the back as on the front. Finely knotted carpets wear better too.

Oriental rugs are really expensive, and I know that old ones can have serious problems. What are these and how should I look for them?
Two quick tips: Hold the rug up to a strong light to look for worn areas and moth holes. You shouldn't be able to see through a good rug. Next, take a handful of rug and gently roll it next to your ear. If it crackles, it's too dry, which means that its fibers won't stand up to being walked on much longer. (And incidentally, one sign of age is flattened knots on the reverse, because if you walk on them, they flatten.)

Cat Paintings

This is a twentieth-century painting. Look at the back of the canvas for age, and sometimes—though not always—the frame.

Light and bright images are usually more desirable than dark ones. Here, the vivid geometry of the rug, the pale gray fur, and the spots of red combine in an almost abstract, and colorful, composition. This kitty brought $5,250.

Unfortunately, this painting is unsigned, but on pictures this appealing, signatures can mean less.

A Little Backstory

Cat paintings are adorable and kitten paintings are adorabler. So getting all those "Awwwws" out of the way up front, we're free to go on to the real point, which is: If you're going to spend your money on a painting—on an original, possibly old, possibly signed oil painting—you'll need to bring more than kitty giddy to the task. There's a real backstory here. Just turn that tabby over to read it.

Good A nice-size picture (20 x 24 inches) of a riveting puss complete with signature, berries, and giltwood frame. What more can you ask for? A little age, maybe. This new Folk Art wannabe sold for $580.

Better Signed and painted by cat painter Brunel de Neuville, this picture has lots of cute cats (better than one cute cat) and charming spools and balls of thread. It's a small painting, however, only 9 × 13 inches, and sold for $3,450, low for this artist.

Best Our top cat is a terrific nineteenth-century American Folk Art painting that has it all: age, bright and colorful imagery, original condition, a fabulous (new) frame, and an adorable, uncutesy feline. It brought $56,000.

Look For

- Signatures on the front, back, or stretcher and exhibition labels. And if you can't quite make out the signature, there are inexpensive Web services that will do that for you.
- Damaged works by listed artists. There is almost no hole, scratch, crease, ding, or undulant canvas that can't be unobtrusively repaired.
- Vintage folk paintings, and even, sometimes, new ones
- Interesting or appropriate framing

Stay Away From

- Large red signatures—these often indicate fakes or reproductions
- Flaking paint, usually the result of a badly prepared surface. Even the best restorers find it a challenge to stabilize flaking paint.
- Paintings on canvases that have been glued down on cardboard
- Paintings that have been overcleaned or overrestored. Today's collectors like their art as is. That way, if they decide to restore it, they know who's done what to it.
- Reliance on artists' names and dates on brass plaques. Be suspicious: Anyone can have anything engraved on a plaque.

Q & A

How can I tell if I'm looking at a real painting and not some kind of convincing brushstroke reproduction?
Here's the aforementioned backstory: Start by turning the painting over. (If the back is covered with paper or cardboard, ask if you can lift one corner to examine the hidden area.) What you should discover there is canvas, artist's board, or wood. Whether the painting itself is an Old Master, from the Victorian era (sweet, sentimental, and dark), or of early twentieth-century origin (sweet, sentimental, and brighter), then the reverse should be age darkened and old. The stretcher (the wood frame to which the canvas is attached) won't have staples, either!

Genuine oil paintings are really, really pricey, aren't they?
Not necessarily. Only signed paintings by listed artists tend to be seriously expensive. If your "talented" aunt Mary did a painting of kitties, it might be just as cute as some big name artist's, but it's also going to be completely affordable (like less than $100). Unless her last name was Cassatt.

I love pictures of cats, but suspect they may be, well, a little kitschy. As painting subjects go, would you say cats are at the high or the low end of the desirability scale?
Academic (that is, highly realistic) cat paintings are accessible and sweet, but in the art world, to be truthful, they rank somewhere below horses and dogs, but above, generally, paintings of little girls with big eyes, and old and toothless men and women (except for old men and women by Rembrandt).

Can a cat painting be a good investment?
While you really should never buy art as an investment, there are times when it might actually be one. Two examples are folk paintings of cats or pictures by artists who specialize in cats. Sadly, there is one nineteenth-century cat painter whose paintings have actually become pricey partially because his increasingly scary images traced the course of his progressive schizophrenia.

Molded top

Nice color

The battens underneath shouldn't extend to edge of top; that would indicate either that the top has been made smaller or that they're not original.

Birdcage

Minimal ornamentation

Sits just a little far back on its snake feet, giving a squatty effect

A Little Backstory

America, like England, was a tea-drinking nation until 1773, when the tea taxes of George III provoked our Boston Tea Party and turned us, possibly forever, into a nation of coffee drinkers. We've never lost our affection, however, for the classic tea table with its circular top, columnar support, and three outsplayed legs. And we'll pay a good deal more for an American table than we will for an English one (though the Brits, like us, prefer their own). American aficionados, in fact, are so eagle-eyed that they can tell the difference between a Philadelphia foot, a New York foot, and a Boston foot—connoisseurship to a, um, T.

Q & A

All the tables in these pictures are mahogany. Is that important to price?

Mahogany, imported from Cuba or Jamaica, was the status wood of the eighteenth century. Its rich, brown-red coloration lent itself to being beautifully carved, it had elegant figuring, and it also took a polish well. In America, fine examples were made in urban centers like New York, Philadelphia, and Newport. But in our "provinces," tables were fashioned from local woods, such as maple or cherry, and are often exceptionally beautiful. Despite not being mahogany, they're equally popular with collectors today.

What do tea tabletops look like?

The best tabletops were constructed from a single board with superlative wood grain. There are square tops, scalloped tops, and hexagonal or octagonal tops.

But what about condition?

In the twentieth century particularly, both American and English tea tables were automatically refinished. Buyers wanted their antiques to look like new. Fortunately, many American tables have been subjected to benign neglect, and these are the tables—ink-stained, dented, scratched, and topped by a satisfyingly nasty waxy buildup—that collectors pay a premium for today.

Look For

- The differing shapes in the ball-and-claw foot that tell advanced collectors in which state—and sometimes city!—the table was made
- "Dished" or molded top edges—along with being ornamental, these kept the tea things from falling off the table!
- Piecrust or scalloped tops
- Carved knees
- Ball and claw feet, especially those on which the talons stand clear of the ball (light will be visible between the two.)
- Labeled or signed eighteenth- and early nineteenth-century tables
- Good labeled Colonial Revival copies from the 1920s to 1930s, which are themselves having a sort of revival

Stay Away From

- Lots of visible repairs
- Poor quality, lightweight reproductions
- Shiny "piano" finishes
- Carving that seems stiff or awkwardly executed
- Tops and tripod bases that weren't "born together"

Good A really nice little mahogany table that appears to have everything: a delicate (and still intact) openwork gallery around its octagonal top, a carved pedestal and carved knees, ball-and-claw feet, and good proportions. It's mid-twentieth century, though, so it has everything except that all-important age. At $190, however, it's a good, decorative buy.

Better This undistinguished tilt-top table has what dealers call a nice surface (it looks old and unrefinished). Its locking mechanism allows the table to tip, and the columnar shaft is fairly skinny in comparison with those substantial legs. The $525 price seems fair.

Best Here's a beautiful table, circa 1765, that has it all: a wonderful provenance, having been sold in the past by *two* of the premiere dealers in American furniture; exceptional carving; gutsy ball-and-claw feet; and best of all, the chalk signature of its Newport maker on the underside of the top. No wonder it brought $60,000!

Silver Cream Pitchers

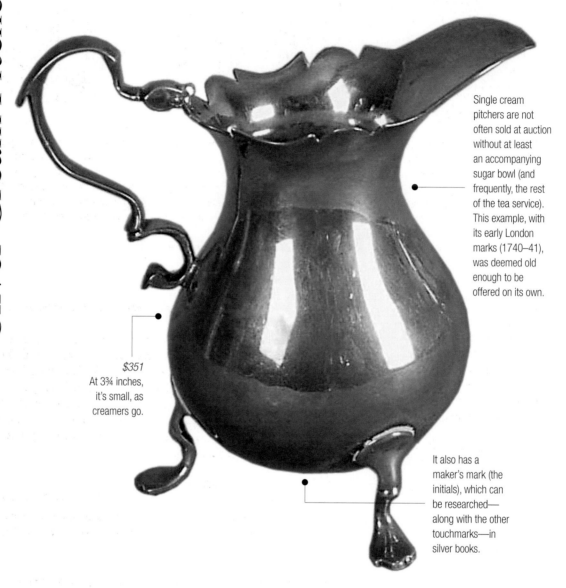

Single cream pitchers are not often sold at auction without at least an accompanying sugar bowl (and frequently, the rest of the tea service). This example, with its early London marks (1740–41), was deemed old enough to be offered on its own.

$351
At 3¾ inches, it's small, as creamers go.

It also has a maker's mark (the initials), which can be researched—along with the other touchmarks—in silver books.

A Little Backstory

Silver cream pitchers are sort of a dime a dozen. Today, we're so used to the idea of cream-and-sugar twins that a single pitcher seems to us to be something of an orphan. You can probably find one for $50 or so. The examples that follow, however, are unusual in several respects, some of them surprising.

Good This attractive octagonal pitcher, 5 inches tall with a floral engraved surface, London date marks for 1845 and a maker's mark, was slightly dented. Perhaps its relatively late date and those dents explain why it brought only $150.

Better Here's a good example of what happens when regional silver is sold in the right venue. Only 4 inches wide and 2 inches tall, this twentieth-century pitcher by well-known Asheville, North Carolina, silversmith William Waldo Dodge came up for sale in Asheville, and brought $600. Had it been offered in Chicago, say, it might have gone unsold.

Best Because of its scenic engraving, age, and maker, this 4¼-inch-high, circa 1745 Jacob Hurd cream jug is rare as hen's teeth. Despite its having an unidentifiable coat of arms, it is one of only six known examples, and sold for $113,525.

Look For

- The marks or names of well-known silversmiths, usually found on the back, the bottom, or bottom edge
- A hammered finish, which can indicate either early silver, or Arts and Crafts–era silver, both desirable
- Russian silver, usually marked "82"
- Colonial-era American silver (remember, Paul Revere was a silversmith)
- Mixed-metal silver in the Aesthetic style. It will be dotted with little copper or brass bugs, fish, reeds, and so on, that have been applied to the silver background

Stay Away From

- Dented silver—the only way to repair a dent is to hammer it out, which thins the metal
- Silver spouts added to mugs (and tankards) to make them into the often more desirable pitchers
- Using a prominently engraved date to judge the age of a piece. It might commemorate an earlier or later event
- Lightweight twentieth-century silver

Q & A

I always thought that weight was the most important thing about sterling silver. How is the weight determined?
Most genuine silver objects are anywhere from 75 percent to 95 percent pure silver, one of the precious—and thus intrinsically valuable—metals. The rest is comprised of other metals that have been added for strength and/or color. American silver—what we call sterling—is generally 950 parts of pure silver in 1000. English sterling is 925/1000, and much of Europe is 800/1000 (which is how you can identify it: It's marked 800). Thus heavier American or English wares actually do have more silver in them than lighter pieces, not to mention pieces that are marked 800.

How do I read indecipherable hallmarks?
Smoke the area around the marks with the flame from a candle—not too close, however! Then press a piece of scotch tape against the smoked area and transfer it to a piece of white paper. You'll have a clear image, ready for your research.

This is a silly question, but why do some silver objects have felt on the bottom?
Many pieces—though not cream pitchers, usually—were routinely weighted. That is, the bases were filled with plaster to keep them from being inadvertently knocked over. This was particularly true of candlesticks, elaborate candelabra, and silver centerpieces. The felt is often there to keep the silver from scratching the table, but also to hide that plaster filler. (A rattling noise in your candlesticks, by the way, means the plaster has broken.) With filled objects, it is impossible to gauge the actual silver weight. Knife handles are filled, and thus are never weighted.

Doorstops

The rarer the form, the higher the price. Our urn full of poppies, at $100 to $200, is relatively inexpensive.

Little chips in the paint are acceptable. However, serious collectors don't buy doorstops with less than three quarters of their original paint.

On painted cast-iron doorstops, the paint should be bright as the day it was applied. This one (you can tell from the overspray) was airbrushed.

The manufacturer's name, if there is one, will be on the bottom or back. This example is by Hubley, which used impressed or incised markings, or a paper label. Old Hubley catalogues reveal that this model was made circa 1946.

Avoid rust. If the manufacturer didn't bother to prime the cast iron, it will rust, and over time bleed through.

A Little Backstory

Do you really *need* a doorstop? Only when the groceries are coming in, possibly, or the movers are going out; when your house needs a little fresh air; when the door between the kitchen and dining room swings shut just as you're coming through with the soup; or when the screen door (remember screen doors?) slams too fast. Truth is, you *do* need a doorstop, especially a good-looking one.

Good This iron example was originally painted gold to emulate the more expensive brass. Its design is vague and generic, but its handle makes it easy to move around. On a really good day, it might bring $50.

Better According to the acid-etched signature centering its well-polished concave bottom, this six-pound glass doorstop was made by Steuben. With its controlled bubbles and attractive blue threads, it's something of a rarity. It retails for $595.

Best Animal forms are popular as doorstops. This English-made Labrador dates from around 1880. Its fur and face have been realistically rendered and hand chased—choice details that haven't been polished away. It retails for $3,500.

Look For

- The impressed initials or names of manufacturers—some better-known makers are the Albany Foundry Company, Bradley & Hubbard, and Hubley
- Doorstops copyrighted by known designers, cartoonists, or artists
- Related cast-iron items, such as book-ends, tiebacks, and window shade pulls
- Dog doorstops still wearing their original leashes (from the 1930s)

Stay Away From

- Suspiciously perfect paint—repainting old doorstops must have been a great temptation for little girls on rainy afternoons
- Rusty doorstops—there's no stopping rust
- Reproductions, identifiable by ill-fitting seams, Phillips-head screws, rough or pebbly surfaces. Don't forget to check for wear.
- Doorstops with chalky-looking paint—they've been washed with hot water
- "Doorstops" that are actually bookends, always shorter and lighter in weight

Q & A

Why go out and buy a doorstop? Won't almost anything hold the door open?
Sure. A handy chair's okay, for example, and so is a potted plant, not to mention a well-placed book, brick, or foot. But bricks and books aren't very pretty, and chairs can be awkward. Brass, on the other hand, is attractive and sturdier than a foot, as is painted cast iron.

Will I have to spend a lot for one?
Today's vintage doorstops were once sold for pennies in gift shops or Sears, Roebuck catalogues, but the relatively new designation "collectible" has made everything expensive, and humble doorstops aren't excepted, certainly not when you can pay $3,000 for a painted cast-iron giraffe or $3,500 for a heron Paradoxically, it was the brass, copper, and nickel-plated kinds that were initially the most expensive. Today, however, we like paint.

I'll bet those high prices mean there are reproductions too.
Absolutely. Vintage painted doorstops are cast iron, meaning that molds can easily be made for recasts. (In fact, during the nineteenth and early twentieth centuries, at the peak of their popularity, that's just how manufacturers copied one another's wares.)

So how do I know which genuine ones to buy?
Try not to be influenced by the fact that your neighbor collects nautical doorstops or windmills or golfers. Then, depending on what attracts *you,* try to find out if it's a highly popular example (read pricey) or not. If no one else is buying nickel-plated sailfish, for example, there will be lots more for you, while those rare giraffes will be, well, rare. You can check prices in books or online. And if you *love* those sailfish, buy them.

The top is perfectly plain mahogany: no marble, no inlay.

The center column is also quite plain, with no carving, although it's encircled at its base by a gilt-metal band, a sophisticated touch.

The lion's-paw feet, when compared with those on the "best" table, seem unnecessarily skimpy. Original casters are usually a plus. It brought $1,392.

A Little Backstory

American Empire tables (like almost every bit of American furniture made until the end of the nineteenth century) were based on English and Continental originals. Fashionable American women, those who could afford to buy and wear Paris gowns, brought what was happening abroad to their own drawing rooms, from which design filtered down. New York and Philadelphia were home to French-influenced designers Charles-Honoré Lannuier and Anthony Quervelle, but Duncan Phyfe fully deserves his long-lived reputation. He was the only furniture manufacturer to develop something of a uniquely American style.

Q & A

Most of what I think of as American Empire is sort of clunky. Do people really collect it?

It was far more popular between 1960 and 1985 than it is today. During those years, much new scholarship was being published, with the Metropolitan and other American museums actively buying Federal and Empire furniture. That gave the best examples a market boost, and the "clunkers" followed in their wake.

How do I tell if a table is American?

English tables are generally more sophisticated than ours, in both design and proportion. Our tables can seem heavy and badly proportioned compared to theirs, but in fact, we *were* the provinces. Many American tables have gold-stenciled ornamentation, for instance, instead of gilded bronze mounts; they'll also sit on crudely carved lion's paw feet instead of on delicate gilt casters.

What is the pillar and scroll style?

The Empire style lasted longer in America than it did in most of Europe, and as it began to peter out circa 1830 to 1845, it became heavier. Instead of being embellished with carving and gilding, American tables metamorphosed into very masculine, all-veneered pieces that retained their classical motifs, but these had metamorphosed into massive S scrolls, C scrolls, or pillars.

Look For

- Rosewood tables
- Brass inlay and/or bronze mounts
- Dolphins, either as feet or supports
- Caryatids, preferred by Lannuier
- Thick marble tops in black or white marble
- Marble supports
- Stenciling
- Labels and branded names

Stay Away From

- Replaced (thin) marble (unless the rest of the table is remarkable)
- Poorly detailed carving
- Overly elaborate design—this is atypical of American Empire.
- Top- or bottom-heavy proportions
- Table bases with legs were less popular here than abroad. America liked the column.
- Refinished tables

Good Some overly ambitious carver lavished much attention on the base of this center table. It's a form frequently seen on card tables as well, and the stuff of collectors' nightmares. The top, however, with its mahogany veneered apron and original marble top, is perfectly nice, and this piece certainly couldn't be made for $1,374 today.

Better A perfect example of late Empire pillar and scroll, this very substantial table, probably made in Boston circa 1850, is quite sophisticated in its own way. The shaped top, the black and gold portoro marble, the coved apron, the circular boss that centers the lower shelf all add to its general elegance. A fine example of a none-too-beloved style, it brought a solid $4,680.

Best Attributed to Philadelphia cabinetmaker Anthony Quervelle, this elegant circa 1820 center table has it all: beautiful proportions, an inlaid top of ebony and satinwood, touches of gilt on the pedestal, and handsomely figured mahogany. It sold for $19,200.

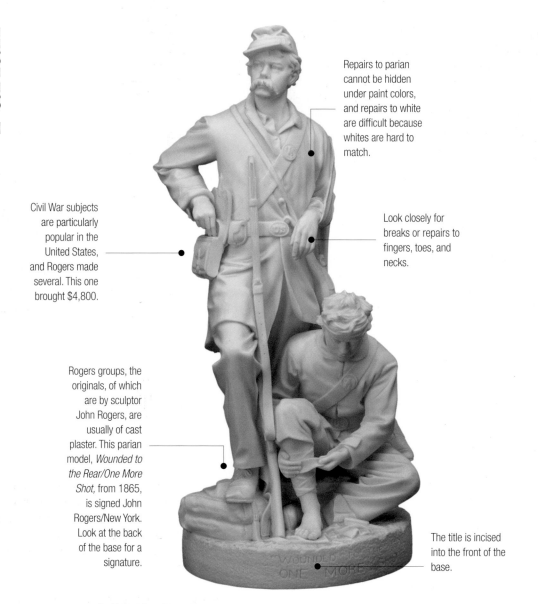

Parian

Repairs to parian cannot be hidden under paint colors, and repairs to white are difficult because whites are hard to match.

Civil War subjects are particularly popular in the United States, and Rogers made several. This one brought $4,800.

Look closely for breaks or repairs to fingers, toes, and necks.

Rogers groups, the originals, of which are by sculptor John Rogers, are usually of cast plaster. This parian model, *Wounded to the Rear/One More Shot,* from 1865, is signed John Rogers/New York. Look at the back of the base for a signature.

The title is incised into the front of the base.

A Little Backstory

Developed in mid-nineteenth-century England to resemble marble, parian is an unglazed, smooth, matte, white ceramic. Unlike bisque, parian doesn't stain, and unlike plaster, it isn't easily broken. (Nor does it dissolve in water!) In Victorian America, every house with any pretension to culture had a parian bust, a sculpture of a statesman, a Greek goddess (much less often a god), or a copy of some popular statue. Today, these are mainly of interest to historians, ceramics scholars, and parian collectors.

Q & A

What is it that keeps parian from staining?

It's made with more feldspar than regular porcelain and it's fired at a lower temperature. Much parian also has a smear glaze, created by putting a pot of glaze into the kiln and volatizing it. This both protected the parian "skin" and supplemented the marble effect.

I think I've seen some examples that are painted in colors or gold. Is that legitimate or was it done later?

Minton, Copeland, and perhaps a few other English manufacturers occasionally painted hair and clothing details on statues. The colors are always very delicate — pale blues, pinks, and yellows with touches of gilding — and a far cry from the breathtakingly bold colors we now know to have been common on ancient Greek marbles.

Why does there seem to be so much parian around?

For about thirty years, from 1850 to 1880, it was retailed by both English and American manufacturers as an "artistic" material. A piece of parian on the mantel was proof that you were a person of some culture and refinement. And it was somewhat costly when it was new, so it also indicated that you were a person of means.

Look For

- Very crisp detailing of costume, hair, hands, and facial features
- Marked American parian
- Sports figures
- Pieces that are known to have been exhibited at one of the international exhibitions — those catalogues are often available in large libraries.

Stay Away From

- Facial hair (on male busts, of course)
- Overly sentimental subjects
- Mushy, ill-delineated features
- Too many firing imperfections, such as black spots or firing cracks, especially when the subject isn't desirable or rare
- The usual chips and cracks

Good Here is an 18-inch marked and dated figure by Copeland, based on a model by William Brodie and dated 1858, which sold for only $237. Undoubtedly, that price wasn't because of the chip to the edge of shawl or the light hairline cracks on the base, but because the subject, *Storm,* is too sentimental for twenty-first-century tastes.

Better Signed Broome, 1876, this 9 ¾-inch portrait bust of Ulysses S. Grant has the advantage of having been made and signed by the finest modeler at the Lenox company. Today, ironically, the reputations of the artist and manufacturer may outweigh that of the subject. It sold for $1,600.

Best A 16 ¾-inch high Belleek figure of Erin (Ireland) with an Irish harp, circa 1875, is unveiling an urn inscribed "Belleek Pottery." Wow! She's in very good condition, but in any condition, Belleek collectors—or Irishmen, for that matter—would fight to own her. Which is probably why she brought $6,518 against a $800 to $1,200 estimate.

Its provenance is impeccable because it comes from a known and well-respected collection. With early furniture, such information can be particularly important. Attractive (and original) details add to value.

This chest is missing its bottom boards and has a replaced top, which is often the case with Pilgrim-era chests. They're rare enough, though, that collectors don't always mind.

Its design says it's seventeenth-century Massachusetts, and even attributable to a known cabinetmaker in Dedham.

A Little Backstory

Pilgrim furniture doesn't really date from 1620, the year of the landing at Plymouth Rock. It's a furniture style that was actually an American adaptation of English Jacobean, which lasted, here, into the 1700s.

We copied everything English, actually, but for furniture we had to use American woods, of course, and because our homes were small, there wasn't much room for large pieces. That's why most of the case furniture that has come down to us consists of Bible boxes and lift-top chests with one or two drawers below. Judging from the numbers that exist, there wasn't an American home that didn't have one.

Q & A

Do we know what these chests were used for?

Many of them were dower chests, made to hold the blankets, handmade linens, and fancy towels that a well-brought-up bride brought to her marriage. In fact, when you find them with initials carved into the central panel, they're generally those of that long-ago bride.

Is there any good way to tell how old they are?

The chest with a lift-top and a drawer or two was the direct descendant of the six-board box, and it appeared in America sometime around 1650. It was so simple to make (stiles and rails form the frame, then panels are inserted, usually three in front and one on each side) that it was still being made in rural areas for years—even as late as 1725.

What woods were they made of?

The outside of the chest is customarily made of oak, a very hard wood popular during the seventeenth century. Oak is a yellow-brown shade when newly cut, but it ages almost to black, and wears to a satisfying smoothness. Within such chests, the hidden elements were frequently pine, and many Pilgrim-era chests were painted red, blue, and black. Some had decorative black-painted split spindles and egg shapes applied to the front.

Look For

- Hand-forged wrought iron nails
- Original hinges, which will *look* handmade
- Original paint, soft and dry to the touch, and often crackled. If no paint is visible, take a closer look for traces remaining in the grain.
- Pieces that have an identifiable place of manufacture, such as Hadley chests, known to have been made in Hadley, Massachusetts, or Guilford, Connecticut, chests
- Vigorous carving, which is a kind of Folk Art
- Unaltered pieces, which are rare because the tops of the chests have often warped and split and been replaced—water rots feet and also lowers the height of drawers.

Stay Away From

- Deceptively well-made copies, many manufactured by Wallace Nutting in the 1920s and 1930s. (These will show the concentric bands of a circular saw, and while constructed of appropriate woods, these are thinner than they should be and lacking in period tool marks.) Handwork—you're looking for evidence of handwork.
- Chests with labels. Labels are a rather recent development.
- Added carving. Original carving was shallow. Fakers found that it was easy (and profitable) to add carving to otherwise plain early chests. Always consult an expert if you're unsure.

Good With its split balusters, three carved sunflowers, and attractively aged appearance, this might be mistaken for a rare Connecticut sunflower chest. The seller, however, listed it as nineteenth century, and the buyers agreed. It brought only $1,912.

Better This American Jacobean chest, known to have been in furniture historian Wallace Nutting's own collection, and illustrated in his famous *Furniture Treasury,* was advertised as being from the Pilgrim era. It sold for $5,250 and looks to have been—uh-oh—refinished.

Best Interestingly, this handsome oak and pine blanket chest, with its applied moldings, spindles and bosses, was pictured in a 1928 *House Beautiful* magazine, and Nutting also illustrated it in his *Furniture of the Pilgrim Century.* Made sometime between 1650 and 1700, it's well worth the $128,000 it sold for.

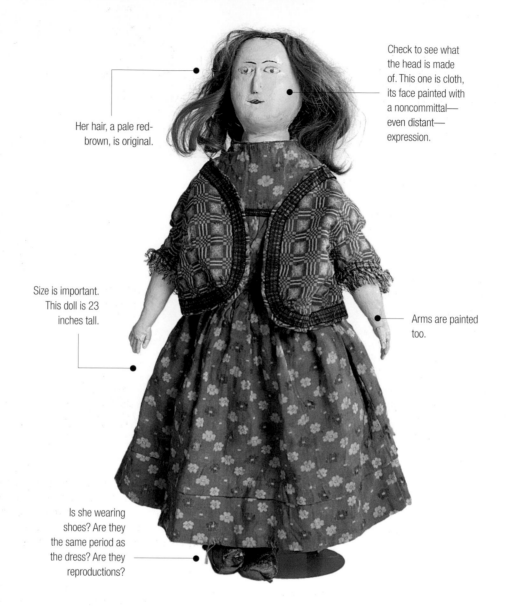

Check to see what the head is made of. This one is cloth, its face painted with a noncommittal— even distant— expression.

Her hair, a pale red-brown, is original.

Size is important. This doll is 23 inches tall.

Arms are painted too.

Is she wearing shoes? Are they the same period as the dress? Are they reproductions?

A Little Backstory

American dolls of this era are a good deal less sophisticated than their European counterparts. With the exception of a few makers (Martha Chase, Izannah Walker, and Ludwig Greiner among them), many of the surviving dolls seem to be of the homemade sort. A number of Native American dolls have survived as well, although they are part of what is known in the world of collectibles as a crossover field. This means that they are sought after by both doll collectors and collectors of Native Americana.

Q & A

What are American dolls made of?

Dolls are primarily characterized by the material their heads are made of. Many are made of cloth—that soft, unbreakable, inexpensive, and natural medium that was easily come by, no matter how far west one went. Others are wood, with painted faces, and still others have painted china heads with molded hair.

Are they more or less valuable than European dolls?

Despite the fact that France and Germany made the most beautiful dolls, American buyers are chauvinists. We're willing to pay a premium for the playthings of our own ancestors.

How can I tell if a doll is American?

Apart from dolls of the makers mentioned above and a few others, it can be difficult, especially with those that are less complex and more like Folk Art. New England–carved wood dolls will look pretty much the same as dolls carved in England, and scholars are always learning more. Perhaps one of the best methods, where the doll isn't identifiably a Walker or a Chase doll, is its provenance. Some beautifully intact old dolls have been handed down through generations, and that pedigree is part of their authentication.

Look For

- China-head dolls with brown eyes
- China-head dolls with a red line above the lid
- Greiner dolls, which have cloth bodies and leather arms, papier-mâché heads with painted (not glass) eyes, and the stamp Patent Head, or Greiner Patent Head
- Papier-mâché in perfect condition (it ages badly)
- Dolls, and especially Folk Art dolls, with a provenance
- Nineteenth-century kachina dolls, which were kept for use by Arizona's Hopis only
- Adult dolls, which predate 1880

Stay Away From

- Replaced heads
- Repaired china heads
- Mismatched heads and bodies
- Reproduction nineteenth-century china-head (and other) dolls
- Dolls in poor condition

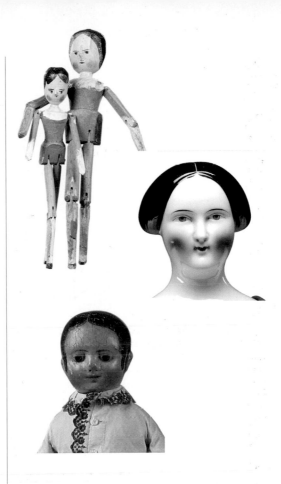

Good

Two "penny" dolls (the name is self-explanatory), one 10 inches and the other 12 inches high, and neither with clothes, sold for $190. Their parted-in-the-middle hair styles mark them as mid-nineteenth-century playthings, and their jointed limbs are put together with wooden pegs. Notice the painted red shoes.

Better

Standing a full 2 feet tall, this glazed porcelain "shoulder head" doll looks like Miss Melly in *Gone With the Wind,* and dates to the Civil War era. Her body is not the original stuffed muslin, but a reproduction with white leather arms. There is little wear to the paint on her hair and face, and she has the red-lined eyelids typical of the period. Her fine condition helped her sell for $1,380.

Best

At 16 inches in a beautiful dress and with a documented descent from the Walker family, this cloth doll sold for $17,625. American collectors are more than willing to pay for rarities, especially those with little wear (just a bit to the hair and a scuff on one cheek) and the perfect provenance.

Globes

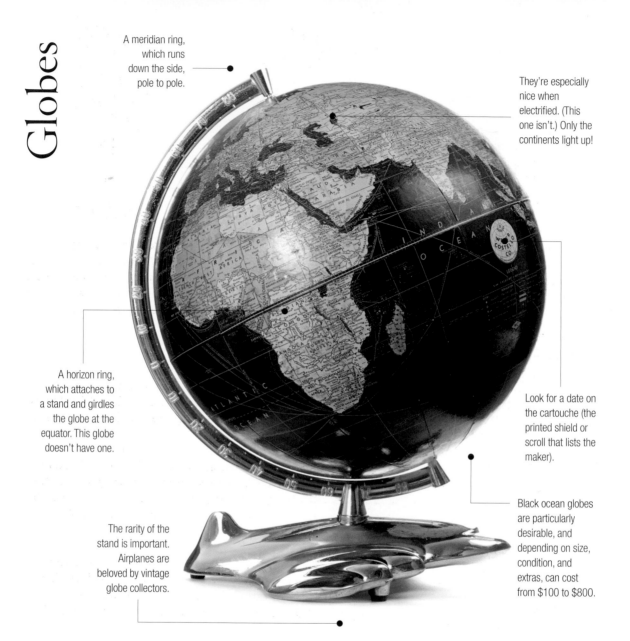

A meridian ring, which runs down the side, pole to pole.

They're especially nice when electrified. (This one isn't.) Only the continents light up!

A horizon ring, which attaches to a stand and girdles the globe at the equator. This globe doesn't have one.

Look for a date on the cartouche (the printed shield or scroll that lists the maker).

The rarity of the stand is important. Airplanes are beloved by vintage globe collectors.

Black ocean globes are particularly desirable, and depending on size, condition, and extras, can cost from $100 to $800.

A Little Backstory

A ball on a stand is an eye-catching bauble. A twirling ball on a stand is a delightful toy. A twirling ball on a stand that is useful, has vintage style and educational value, and is decorative is a globe. And collectible globes—as table ornaments, floor models, or pocket-sized conveniences—are always out-of-date but also timeless, the best of all possible worlds.

24 ■ Carol Prisant

Good In the Depression era, transfer-printed globe-form children's tin banks encouraged neighborliness. This homely 4-inch globe, if perfect, might bring $95. With dents and surface losses, it's only $65.

Better A mere 6 inches in diameter, this wooden Hammond globe has a green-patinated bronze base. The shellac coating has yellowed the oceans, but that Art Deco base puts it in the $550 range.

Best Also 6 inches, this little globe is valued at $1,500 because it's old (nineteenth century), because its French manufacturer is uncommon, because its colors are fresh, but primarily because it's decorative.

Look For

- "Full mount" globes, easily identifiable by all their trimmings: an equatorial ring around the center, the vertical meridians attached to the stand, and maybe—if you're lucky—a fancy finial
- Figural stands—airplanes, for example
- Globes on which the oceans are rendered in black instead of blue. The rarest of all are those with silver, or even gold, oceans.
- Slate globes, which are not only rare but enormously heavy. An 8-inch example might weigh forty pounds.

Stay Away From

- Student globes made of 6-inch cardboard on cheap wire stands.

Q & A

Where do vintage globes come from?
Kids' rooms and schoolrooms had globes, usually table models, but so did libraries, which generally had space enough for impressive floor globes. During the last century, you might have found either type in home libraries or studies.

How can I tell how old a globe is?
Until around 1900, the date of manufacture was usually printed right on it. But for anything after that, collectors have to hit the (history) books and the Web. When you discover that Persia became Iran in 1935, for instance, or that Indian Territory didn't become Oklahoma (with that fabulous song) until 1907, you'll have narrowed your dates.

I have a globe with what looks like one label pasted on top of another. What is that?
Many of our American globe makers (most of which were based in Chicago) purchased English globes and sold them here under their own labels. Sometimes, the original label or a British emblem peeks out from beneath.

What makes one globe pricier than another?
For twentieth-century globes, it's primarily the stands. Collectors are partial to those from the 1930s to the early 1950s because these seem most stylish. Wooden stands, incidentally, frequently reflect the furniture style of the period in which they were made—English Regency, for example, or Art Nouveau.

Is there more than one type of globe?
The one you'll come across most often is terrestrial, but there are celestial globes too. They were sometimes sold in pairs.

Audubon Prints

Does the image have its margins? This one does.

Fading of colors decreases value, as do creases.

This chromo-lithograph, an 1860 version, brought $10,625.

Audubon's owls are not as popular as his pretty birds. The giant pink ones, for example, the flamingos, are more popular than, say, sparrows.

Discoloration of the paper shouldn't impinge on the image, and neither should foxing.

Look for tears at the edges. Small ones, that don't touch the image, are allowable.

A Little Backstory

When you buy a print, you buy a genuine artist-created work on paper. The image you own has also been printed a number of times, because prints are multiples. And there are numerous techniques for making prints: etching, woodblock, engraving, lithograph, silkscreen, to name just a few. There can also be as many of a single image—twenty-five, say, or two hundred or two thousand—as the artist chose to print. That's why you need to buy the best example you can find—and afford.

Good This example of Audubon's Little Owl is a reduction of the original. This full sheet of paper measuring 23½ × 15½ inches, is smaller than the original and water stained. It brought $250.

Better The paper size is right (38 × 24¾ inches) and it has the requsite J Whatman watermark. But it's not a spectacular or popular image. It brought $1,000.

Best This is one of Audubon's few night scenes. With no stains, only one tiny marginal tear, and negligible surface soiling—size is also right—38¼ x 24¾ inches. This spectacular image sold for $122,500.

Look For

- Popular prints by known artists: George Bellows's *Between Rounds* or *Stag at Sharkey's*, for example
- Eighteenth- and nineteenth-century sporting prints
- Good, colorful botanicals
- Rembrandts, Goyas, and Van Dycks— all have not only been extensively reproduced, but the artists' original plates were also printed over and over, degrading the original, crisp images. Homework first!

Stay Away From

- Foxing (that brownish freckling on the paper, although it *can* be safely removed)
- Trimmed margins, where the original edges of the paper—to enable the print to fit within a frame or because of soiling—have been cut off right up to, or even within, the image
- Touched-up colored engravings (called aquatints), which were printed in colors, then further painted by hand. Some have been recolored in modern times.
- Tears and mends to the paper
- Faded color. *Warning:* Keep all prints away from sunlight.

Q & A

How can I tell a genuine print from a photo reproduction of a print?
Many prints are pressed into paper, and the printing block leaves its mark. So look for an impression of that rectangular block a few inches within the paper's margins. (If the print is framed up to the image, ask to see it out of the frame.) Modern prints are usually signed in pencil. But take a magnifying glass to the surface of the print. If little pixels of color are visible under magnification, you're looking at some sort of reproduction—and usually, it's of a well-known or costly work on paper (another name for prints).

Are all prints signed and numbered?
Only twentieth- and twenty-first-century prints. Those from the eighteenth and nineteenth centuries can have, in very fine lettering just beneath the image, the name of the artist, the engraver, and/or the publisher. Very early prints will be on handmade paper.

And what do those penciled numbers mean?
One number, the larger one, refers to the number of prints the artist has decided to produce from his copper plate, wood block, or lithograph. If he's made two hundred copies, then yours might be numbered 46/200. It's the forty-sixth image taken from his plate or block or stone. The letters "AP" stand for "artist's proof," the one or more test pieces he "pulls" before beginning the actual print run.

Are prints ever as expensive as paintings?
If an artist's style translates beautifully into the print format, such as Chagall's, for example, it might actually bring more than an oil painting (though not Chagall's!).

Sterling Napkin Rings

The rolled edges look substantial and solid, not hollow.

Makers are important. This napkin ring, which brought $350, is marked Tiffany & Co.

The edges of the applied oak leaf border have been polished down somewhat, but not enough to have lost definition.

Even from a photo, you can sense the weight of this silver.

A Little Backstory
Toward the end of the nineteenth century, the growing popularity of the lavishly set table meant that silver manufacturers could add one more completely necessary item to their list of tablewares: napkin rings. These could be as plain or elaborate as the market would bear, and could be purchased in sets of a dozen or as a pair for newlyweds. Not as popular as figural napkin rings, good examples are still in demand.

Q & A

How do I tell silver from silverplate?
To begin with, there are marks. American-made silver is marked with the word "sterling." English silver will have hallmarks that can be easily found in books on silver. (Beware, however, of the dreaded EPNS, which stands for electroplated nickel silver.) Plated napkin rings will usually be heavier than sterling, as well.

But what if it's marked "sterling" and is really heavy?
Check carefully on the edges inside the ring for maker's marks. Tiffany & Co. and Gorham are two American manufacturers that offered unusually heavy silver wares. Tiffany, in fact, had four weights for flatware, and buyers of the Chrysanthemum or Audubon silver patterns, for instance, could indicate which weight they preferred. Heavy sterling napkin rings are more desirable than lightweight ones.

There are auctions where there are twenty or thirty unmatched napkin rings selling together and "melt value" is mentioned. What is that?
Silver is a precious metal. As such, it has intrinsic value. With the advent of the paper napkin, individual napkin rings have become less popular than they were in the Belle Epoque era (circa 1870–1914), and unless there is something particularly beautiful or interesting about them, they are considered to be worth only the value of their silver, melted down.

Look For

- Elegant and heavy Tiffany napkin rings
- Examples in "mixed metal," an Aesthetic era technique in which the silver was decorated with applied insects or flora in copper and brass. Tiffany experimented with this method for a short while.
- Your own, or your family monogram on sets of rings, which is fun for holiday tables
- Kalo wares, from the Chicago silver shop of that name

Stay Away From

- Individual lightweight napkin rings (unless they have some personal significance)
- Dented rings, a common problem
- Napkin rings on which the rolled silver edges are split

Good Perhaps because they are handsomely decorated, or heavier than the usual, these rings commanded $270. This set of seven engraved early twentieth-century English napkin rings (one in silver plate) more than tripled its low estimate, yet made less than $50 each. Perhaps two bidders really just wanted them!

Better Children's silver—cups, porringers, pap boats, and napkin rings—are perennially collectible. This unmarked 1-inch-wide napkin ring from late in the nineteenth or early in the twentieth century is acid etched with a scene of youngsters in a garden. Encircling the top and bottom is a verse. It brought $125.

Best This very simple pair of silver ribbon–form napkin rings was made by Kalo, the Chicago-based maker of hand-wrought silver tablewares and jewelry. In production from the early to mid-twentieth century, Kalo items—even those with applied monograms—are highly sought after by American collectors. These sold for $360.

Windsor Chairs

There are perhaps a dozen different styles of Windsor chair: sack backs, hoop backs, and continuous-arm brace-backs—like this one—among them.

Although most Windsors were painted, this example shows no traces at all of old paint and so, perhaps, never was.

Gutsiness and artistry in arm curvatures and leg turnings are good indications of quality.

We know this is a New York chair because, just below the pommel of the seat, it was stamped by its listed maker.

Look for wear in appropriate places: on the feet and hand rests especially, but also on the top rail, which has often been dusted smooth or dinged.

The legs of this New York chair have a rare, exaggerated splay, giving it enormous character.

A Little Backstory

Was Ben Franklin sitting in a Windsor chair when he came to the dubious conclusion that our national bird should be the turkey? In honor of that possibility, here are a few words about . . . the chair.

It's a graceful, practical chair—comfortable, light (and therefore, portable), elegant in its simplicity, at home in every setting, and a felicitous emblem of our noble past. The Windsor chair is an all-purpose chair and, unquestionably, no turkey.

Good This comb-back chair, with clumsy proportions, graceless paddle arms, and top-rail "ears" is badly finished. Made of yew, it's English too, and less interesting to U.S. collectors.

Better This nineteenth-century Pennsylvania comb-back was a pretty good chair until someone decided to spiff it up with a lot of white and burgundy paint. At $2,900 you'd probably want to strip it.

Best With handsomely turned splayed legs, delicate, curved armrests, and a slender, sophisticated crest rail, this superbly proportioned Nantucket fanback is worth every cent of $17,000.

Look For

- Rocking chairs. Rockers are common additions to old chairs, but original rockers have thicker-than-ordinary legs.
- Spindles that look whittled, not machined
- Original paint, or traces of old paint where arms, legs, or spindles are joined to the seat
- Revolving chairs, invented by the Shakers
- Windsor chairs with writing arms

Stay Away From

- Chairs with mechanically perfect turnings. These are generally indicative of reproductions.
- Seats made from more than a single piece of wood, the mark of a new chair
- Carefully finished seat bottoms. Old craftsmen left them relatively rough.
- Fancy spindles on continuous-arm armchairs.
- Recent paint, which might be used to disguise replaced parts or repairs
- Cut-down legs. Water damage and wear could make legs uneven. One solution was to cut them down.

Q & A

What makes a good Windsor chair?
Engineering, because a good Windsor is properly engineered. It's made of solid, thoughtfully chosen wood—several kinds, usually, with pine or poplar for the seat, maple for sturdy legs, and ash to bend easily into continuous arms and backs. Old chairs were painted to disguise their mismatched woods.

Painted? Then I guess it's important that the paint be original?
If there's one thing we've all learned from *Antiques Roadshow,* it's that "original surface" is important. Untouched original paint is a real plus. (It didn't used to be that way. In the first three quarters of the twentieth century, when so many antiques got "freshened up," old paint got stripped.)

There seem to be a lot of Windsors around. How can I tell if a chair is antique?
Windsor chairs first showed up in seventeenth-century Britain and then, like everything English, migrated to America. A 1920s chair handcrafted in rural Kentucky can look like an 1806 Connecticut chair or a 2010 New York chair (though seldom like an English chair). Because the style has been popular for so long, they're *very* hard to date.

I've heard that maker's marks increase value, but what's the likelihood of my finding one?
Maker's marks definitely enhance the value of antique furniture and appear—when they do appear—in chalk, ink, pencil, or as brands, often under chair seats (after about 1825, they're likely to be stenciled. Early furniture wasn't often signed, though, in part because many early craftsmen had religious scruples about vanity. Yet even when an old chair isn't "signed," its design details (a certain style of leg or arm) tell us if it's Rhode Island, Pennsylvania, or New York.

Run your finger around the rim to check for chips or repairs.

Is the piece large? This one is 10¾ inches.

Is the painting skillful?

Are the colors pretty or are they representative of the Arts and Crafts era? (The latter can be an advantage too.)

Check the bottom for a maker's mark and perhaps a signature. This piece is cryptically marked, "AA."

Twentieth-Century American Hand-Painted Porcelain

A Little Backstory

The Arts and Crafts, or Craftsman, movement may have been a reaction to the machine-made excesses of Victorian design, a return to the pure, the natural, the handmade. But simultaneously, a vein of femininity continued on, especially in porcelain, which, in its willing-hands-at-home craftsmanship and general dreaminess, seemed just the thing to hold down the shawl on the top of the grand piano. There were handsome and representative Arts and Crafts ceramics, but the following aren't among them.

Q & A

What makes these vases different from earlier ones? Many of those are hand painted too.

Most porcelain created before the Arts and Crafts attempt to reform the decorative arts was distinctly photorealistic. In fact, that was often the whole idea: how realistically that rose or this branch could be painted. Ceramics of this era, while still photorealistic, can often be a little (a *very* little) like Impressionist paintings.

Aren't many of them signed by women?

Actually, while many women painted tablewares at porcelain factories toward the end of the nineteenth century, the era of the Arts and Crafts movement, American porcelain firms such as Willets Belleek sold many blanks (undecorated vases and plates) to individuals or women's clubs that wanted to try their hand at china painting.

But they're so pretty. Why aren't they more popular?

Truthfully? Because they're just a little ditzy. In Arts and Crafts ceramics, much of the important work was shifting away from porcelains to pottery, appreciated for its earthy qualities. Pottery wasn't white, like porcelain, so it lent itself better to the muted hues of the "modern" craftsman movement. Because collectors of this period (and all periods) look to buy things that are most representative of their era, they consider these painted porcelains merely a detour off the main aesthetic highway.

Look For

- Unusually large pieces
- Vases where each side is painted with a different subject
- Signed pieces that are labeled, as well, by notable manufacturers
- Subjects and paintings that complement the shape of the vase

Stay Away From

- Unmarked ceramics
- Poor quality painting
- Murky coloration
- Vases that have been drilled for electricity (they'll have a hole in the bottom)

Good This 13½-inch ewer was painted by an amateur who didn't buy her blank from a known factory (there's no manufacturer's mark on the bottom.) Pleased enough with her effort to sign and date it, she painted her name on the bottom, "Jeanice Nunneley, less '88." No relatives seem to have been among the bidders, and it sold for $70.

Better Just a little larger, but far more interesting, this 16-inch cylindrical vase depicting whooping cranes is both a good subject and is painted in the earthy hues that were so popular in this period. Add to that the fact that it has the Willets Belleek mark on the underside, and it's well worth the $451 it sold for.

Best Valued at $1,600, this very large vase (21 inches) has obviously been painted by a highly accomplished artist. The softly colored roses gracefully wind around its neck and down its side. On the bottom, it is marked with the Willets stamp and a hand-lettered, "France Studio."

Nakashima Coffee Tables

The top of this 15 × 42¾ × 33-inch freeform table is maple burl, a particularly desirable wood.

The edges are quite elaborate.

It is signed and dated on the underside "Geo. Nakashima/Nov 21 '85."

The Minguren I base is oak.

The butterfly is made of rosewood.

A Little Backstory

There's good reason for the renewed popularity of the wood slab coffee table. It's as "green" as furniture can be. It's all about the tree. And an additional halo around the iconic George Nakashima coffee table is that it's also American—and first-rate design. But there are good, better, and best even among things that look amazingly alike. And here's why.

Q & A

Why are Nakashima coffee tables so expensive?
The coffee table is purely a twentieth-century phenomenon, which can't be said of almost any other type of furniture. It resides in a very public room as well, so friends know how tasteful, sophisticated, and, yes, rich, you are. Yet Nakashima tables are studio furniture, made by hand by a talented designer/craftsman. The slabs of wood that constitute these table tops have been hand selected for their beauty, color, and grain. Add to it all the fact that he was an *American* artist (because we are chauvinistic, after all) working in a unique style, and you have a major collectible.

Wouldn't it be fairly easy just to cut down a tree and make my own in the basement?
It would, and it's been done. The problem is that people aren't just buying a wooden coffee table. They're buying the mystique of the lone genius in his wood shop, laboring over his rare materials, believing that his finished product is perfect enough to put his name on. If you're in doubt as to authenticity, though, you can always go to New Hope, Pennsylvania, to have Nakashima's daughter, Mira, authenticate it. Records exist there of all the furniture and, in many instances, the clients it was made for.

Isn't it unusual to have someone around who can authenticate works of art? Does that make buying such things safer?
It does, because it's so rare to have a family member still alive, and one who is knowledgeable and willing to guarantee authenticity. This may very well account, in part, for the unusually high prices of Nakashima cocktail tables. Their pedigree can be checked.

Look For

- Rosewood or maple
- Beautifully figured wood slabs
- Owners' names in something like black magic marker on the underside
- Butterflies (the butterfly-shaped wooden "Band-Aids" that reinforce cracks)
- Signed pieces

Stay Away From

- Any finish other than oil: for example, shellac, varnish, lacquer
- Cigarette burns and alcohol or water rings
- Fakes
- Unauthenticated pieces (unless you've found them at a tag sale for less than $100)

Good This 1970s table top (14 × 65¾ × 18 inches) is walnut, most common of the Nakashima wood slabs, and sold for $24,000. It also has a rosewood butterfly.

Better This walnut table is almost a foot longer (13 x 73 x 20 inches) and has an interesting leading edge and good markings. The designer's early pieces are simpler, because at that point in his career, he couldn't afford the more costly woods. It brought $66,000.

Best Carpathian elm burl makes an exotic and particularly shapely 1975 table top (15¼ × 71½ × 24 inches). The symmetrical base is called Minguren I, and because this example also came with the original bill of sale, correspondence, and has the owner's name in black marker on the bottom it sold for $108,000.

Cocktail Shakers

This shiny threesome is all silver plate. In general, collectors prefer plate to chrome.

These shakers are sixty to seventy years old, but their shapes are quite common. Skyscraper silhouettes and figural shakers are particularly desirable.

Before you buy, check that the parts that ought to come apart *do* come apart, and avoid conspicuous dents.

While unusual features, such as the applied anchor on this nautical-theme shaker, generally add value, the anchor "chain" on this one has come off and been somewhat clumsily reattached.

The Tells-U-How shaker was enormously popular. Rotate the bottom section, and the recipe for each of sixteen cocktails listed on the shoulder appears, ingredient by ingredient, in the slots. The wording should be legible.

The Nautical shaker is $475, the Tells-U-How is $1,800, the one with the chained spout is $485. Prices can be higher around the holiday season (and in the United Kingdom).

Footed shakers will be steadier on their feet.

A Little Backstory

Shaken, not stirred. And with good reason too.
Shaken cocktails aren't just fizzy and mildly dilute, they're festive. And cocktail shakers, like 007, brim with black-tie glamour and retro-chic. Like him, they're sexy too. All flashy gadgetry and solid function, all sleek and shapely and extrasmooth. All elegant symbols of The (very) Good Life, not to mention sophistication. Here's to them. Both.

Good From the 1950s, a glass shaker is encircled in glorious roosters. (Yes, cocktails.) Colorful, it has a chrome lid and sells for $185. If the paint were faded or scuffed, it would bring far less.

Better A midcentury "barbell" in opaque and rich cobalt-blue glass is banded in platinum paint, and uniquely easy (and fun) to shake with one hand. Try this at home for $795.

Best This aristocratic Revere Empire shaker in chrome and Bakelite was designed in 1938 by William Archibald Welden. Its streamlined look is typical of 1930s design. Its $2,750 price is typical of the current cocktail shaker market.

Look For

- Music box shakers that play "How Dry I Am" or similar tunes when lifted
- The penguin with an upper beak that *lifts*. A silver version of this penguin has gilt trim and was more expensive when new. Unsurprisingly, it will be more expensive today.
- Chrome plated shakers with Bakelite trim (in good condition)
- The 1936 Manhattan Skyscraper shaker by industrial designer Norman Bel Geddes
- The complete chrome Ferris Wheel set (glasses, shaker, and "wheel"), also by Bel Geddes

Stay Away From

- Copies made by contemporary firms. Though these work as well as the old ones, collectors prefer vintage.
- Tops and bottoms that aren't original to each other. Check the fit—and reference books.
- Battery-powered shakers. You know, like that cute one with the white-mustachioed bartender who rocks back and forth? (He has his fans, though.)

Q & A

I read about someone who wanted to "invest" in a vintage cocktail shaker. Are they actually investments?

Recently I met a woman who showed me a curious shaker she'd bought at a tag sale for $2. Shaped like a dirigible, it had a "nose" that, when unscrewed, revealed four spoons, a ladle, a funnel, a corkscrew, a juice strainer, four cups, and a decanter. It was a rare 1930s Henckels Zeppelin shaker made in Germany, worth $6,000 or so today.

When were they originally popular?

Prohibition (1920 to 1933) did wonders for alcohol and its accoutrements, but the shaker's golden age was from about 1930 to 1941. After that, World War II created a metal shortage, so they didn't reappear until the 1950s. Collectors look for the early ones, especially if they're figural or sculptural.

Some cocktail shakers have spouts and some don't. Are there different types?

Those with spouts are descendants of coffee pots, a reference to cocktails being served at the hour for afternoon tea. There are two other common models: a two-piece shaker, the Boston, which has a large mixing cup and a smaller press-fit metal cap, and a three-piece version that unscrews at the shoulder *and* at the top, where there's a strainer and cap. The three-piece version is called a cobbler.

How do I keep mine shiny?

You'll find vintage metal cocktail shakers in sterling silver (if you're really, really lucky), silver plate, nickel over brass, aluminum, pewter, and chrome all clean up with metal polish. Some glass shakers have been jollied up with transfer-printed pink elephants or polar bears. Hand wash these, because their decorations will come off in the dishwasher.

Silhouettes

Are there rips or creases in the paper?

Fakes can have anachronisms in clothing.

Continental silhouettes often have fancy printed borders.

Look for an interesting face or costume, or unusual details like nosegays instead of just conventional profiles.

Is the sitter identified and is it dated? This example has that valuable info on the back.

Avoid water-stained paper.

Does the "ghost" of another frame show on the front? If so, the frame has been changed, and though old frames are nice, *original* old frames are nicer; and *decorative* original frames are nicest. This frame is an old one, but a bit of a clunker.

Look for the artist's signature (keeping in mind that "fecit" always means so-and-so "made this." It is not an artist's name). This one is by the noted August Edouart.

A Little Backstory

Before photography, the rich had their portraits professionally painted, but almost anyone (even George III and Catherine the Great were big fans) could afford a silhouette. Fashioned with just paper and scissors, or with coal-black paint, the quickie silhouette could be executed by professional and amateur both, and was the budget way to hang an image of a loved one on the parlor wall. Nowadays, we think they're not just decorative, but soulful somehow, and attractively austere.

Good This American hollow-cut silhouette is set on wrinkly black silk. The image is conventional and the frame is new and, well, cheesy. The $295 price seems fair.

Better An inscription on the back tells us this silhouette was cut in 1851. His coat and pants are painted and his profile pasted on watercolor-washed card that gives him a shadow. That inscription, plus his painted dog, account for its $950 value.

Best Circa 1850, this group silhouette of an American family is neither signed nor dated. Estimated to sell for $2,000 to $3,000, it sold for $114,000, perhaps because of the strong possibility of its being a masterwork by August Edouart.

Look For

- Silhouettes in stark black paint on white plaster; these are among the oldest.
- Groups of all kinds, especially any with painted details of hair or clothing
- Old labels on the backs of frames
- Value-enhancing inscriptions or signatures
- Embellishments, especially painted ones, such as bronzing, a kind of brushed on gilding, and props, such as flowers and animals
- Eighteenth-century American subjects

Stay Away From

- Silhouettes that have been printed, not cut or painted.
- Faked signatures. Keep in mind that old ink turns brown.
- Reproductions, or artificially aged silhouettes, newly housed in pretty antique frames
- Hollow-cut silhouettes on black velvet backgrounds
- Anything, naturally, signed "Jean Millette"

Q & A

Is silhouette collecting still popular? I always thought it was a 1950s hobby.
Absolutely, though most collectors preferred eighteenth- and nineteenth-century silhouettes. There are even collectors who limit themselves to right- or left-facing profiles or to celebrity look-alikes! Talented cutters worked well into the 1930s at vacation spots like Atlantic City, however, and they have a growing fan base today.

Are silhouettes always handmade?
Because the medium was so popular, silhouettists eventually devised various mechanical aids. One was a kind of pantographic device with which the sitter's shadow was traced full size, then mechanically reduced, then cut. Machine-cut examples aren't highly prized, however, so check for impressions in the paper that might have been caused by a pantograph's stylus, for a certain stiffness of outline, and for a giveaway "two-snip" lock of hair on the forehead.

There seem to be so many silhouettes around. Are there a lot of fakes?
Most collectibles aren't faked until fakers can make substantial money. At the height of the late nineteenth-century fashion for collecting silhouettes, hundreds were faked by a still-unidentified artist signing himself Jean Millette. The Metropolitan Museum purchased several.

How do I tell the difference between American silhouettes and those that were done in England or Europe? Are theirs better than ours?
European work can be more elegant, certainly, and it includes both painted and scissored images as well as silhouettes on glass. Here in America, we had mainly cutters, many of whom specialized in hollow-cut profiles scissored from the center of a piece of paper that they then pasted on a dark background. (The brilliant French cutter, August Edouart, worked in America for years.)

Blue Glass

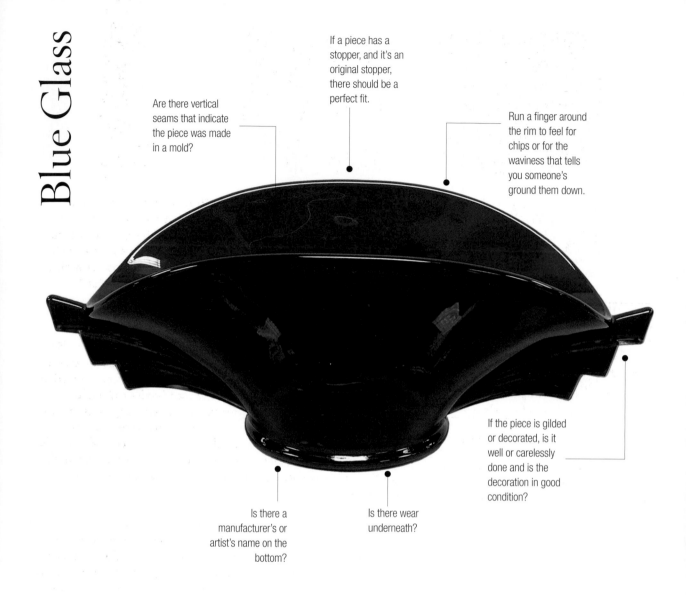

Are there vertical seams that indicate the piece was made in a mold?

If a piece has a stopper, and it's an original stopper, there should be a perfect fit.

Run a finger around the rim to feel for chips or for the waviness that tells you someone's ground them down.

If the piece is gilded or decorated, is it well or carelessly done and is the decoration in good condition?

Is there a manufacturer's or artist's name on the bottom?

Is there wear underneath?

A Little Backstory

Collecting glass takes courage. All those careless movers. All those Frisbees. All those cats. And all those perils that taken together cause most glass collections to wind up in cabinets . . . behind more glass. Blue glass, however, is special. It blooms in sunlight, and blues of every description—aqueous, turquoise, cobalt, and sky—are carefully and endlessly collected.

Good Here's an early twentieth-century 4¼-inch high Bohemian trinket box in blue overlay, cut-to-clear, glass. In perfect condition, bound in brass, it brought $400. Pretty, but unmarked, it's not a "collectible."

Better This iridescent blue-green Blenko decanter set is signed and dated 1969 by Joel Phillip Myers, Blenko design director from 1963 to 1970. Estimated at $2000–$4000, it only brought $800. Fifteen years ago it might have been $80.

Best This mid-nineteenth-century Bohemian blue-overlay 12-inch goblet, signed F. Zach, is engraved with the image of a statue exhibited at the Great Exhibition in London in 1851. It's a document and a work of art, and brought $28,000.

Look For

- The tiny, overlapping scratches that indicate years of wear
- Glass with lead in it pings when tapped; it's only true for bowls or drinking glasses. Glass with smallish necks or openings won't usually ring even if there *is* lead in them.
- Paper labels on vintage glassware (these were often washed off). Check with a magnifying glass for incised signatures too. They can be obscured by those multiple scratches mentioned above.

Stay Away From

- Glass with too many bubbles in it. An indication of age, it is also a distinguishing feature of twentieth-century Mexican reproductions.
- Cracks. There *is* valuable damaged glass but it's either ancient (think Rome) or (very, very, very) old Venetian.
- Worn paint and gilding (a little wear is fine, though). Surface decoration is almost as fragile as glass itself. The makers of 1930s or early Bristol glass, for instance, never imagined the dishwasher. Avoid decorated glass if it's been "dishwashered."

Q & A

Is blue glass rare?
Blue itself isn't rare because the color's so easily made. Simply add metallic oxides, such as cobalt or copper, to colorless silica (sand) and poof—instant blue. But there are so many styles, types, and eras to choose from—American, English, French, Czechoslovakian, blown, pressed, bottles, baskets, boxes, Tiffany, Baccarat, Depression—that certain forms (vases or goblets, maybe) by certain makers will sometimes be rare; or individual pieces have now become rare because they never sold well and so there are fewer of them. The tiny number of extant examples from good factories that never made much blue can be rare too. (And if you're partial to American glass, mold-blown blue is rare indeed!)

How can I tell if a piece is old? (And is that really important anyway?)
Irregularities or waviness around edges or on foot rims or handles *can* mean that glass is old, but it can also mean that my son made it at glass camp. So if you're partial to something pricey like Stiegel-type glassware, which had *better* be old, study up before you buy. On the other hand, if you're simply in love with one celestial shade of blue, then the whole eighteenth to twenty-first centuries are yours and the only time that age will be remotely important is when it seems to be part of the price.

What about damage?
Glass collectors are pretty tough about damage because, almost alone among collectibles, jagged cracks in glass can't be repaired or even concealed. But they do allow a little (very careful) grinding down of small rim chips. (And if you decide to buy cracked examples anyway, either because they're irresistible or because they fill a hole in your collection, refer to these—with a smile—as "cabinet pieces.")

Eighteenth-Century English Porcelain Figures

This early 1750s Chelsea porcelain figure of a parakeet, a mere 4¾ inches in height, sold for $13,200. Why? Only a few such parakeets are known. They were modeled after illustrations in George Edwards's *A Natural History of Uncommon Birds*, though its author deplored their misrepresented shapes and colors. Such figures seem to come on the market every twenty to forty years, which stimulates collectors.

The cocked head adds charm.

Watch for missing bits, especially on beaks and tails. This bird has been repaired, but collectors are willing to accept repairs on real rarities.

The moss on its base seems to identify it as having come from a well-known modeler.

It is marked with Chelsea's raised red anchor.

When figures have no marks, bases are often helpful in identifying the manufacturer.

A Little Backstory

Figures are the great show-offs—the jewelry—of the porcelain world. They're more difficult to make than plates or many vases and, of course, are far less useful. Most were copied from the prints of the day. You'll find eighteenth-century English figures more often in Great Britain than in the United States, and generally speaking, they pay more for them there, every country preferring its own artists. And the English were accomplished ceramicists. What follows is a *very* small sampling.

Good A Bow, c. 1760, troubadour strums an unwieldy lute. The figure is charming and almost 6 inches high, but it's unremarkable and has unspecified restorations. It brought a fair $720.

Better From the same decade, this is a 5-inch Derby grape vendor. Estimated at less than the lutenist, it brought $3,200, perhaps because of his pink coat, those grapes and blossoms, and perfect condition.

Best Dolphins, especially a pair less than 4 inches high, are unusual subjects. Though unmarked, these may be Chelsea porcelain. Both tails have been repaired, but they are still a pair, and an odd subject, and thus worth $8,400.

Look For

- Unusual types of figures, such as wild animals or figures with interesting vocations
- Worcester figures, which are rare
- Press-molded figures. (The exposed interior will be lumpy with the thumbprints left in the clay as it was pressed into the mold.)
- Large figures

Stay Away From

- Figures marked "England" (usually indicating late nineteenth-century manufacture) or "made in England" (indicating anywhere from 1921 to the present)
- Overpainting: a "fix" that extends well beyond the limits of the actual break, and extends what should be a touch-up on a broken wrist, for instance, all the way up the sleeve
- Cracks, which can be artfully hidden. Examine carefully, especially fingers, necks, and flyaway parts, like wings and tails.

Q & A

Who were England's eighteenth-century porcelain manufacturers?
Most are long gone, but some are still in business today: Chelsea, Bow, Longton Hall, Derby, Worcester, Lowestoft, and the first to manufacture hard-paste porcelain, Plymouth.

What is hard-paste porcelain?
The formula for making true, or hard-paste, porcelain was well established in China, but Europeans had to reinvent it. Their earliest efforts resulted in what was called soft-paste porcelain, a material that scratched and chipped far more than the Chinese hard-paste ceramic. At the beginning of the eighteenth century, the Meissen factory in Germany learned the secret—the addition of a clay called kaolin, along with feldspar—and thus were born the tea mugs we use today.

But so many of them look really old.
Porcelain figures have been copied forever, especially with marks of the famous factories. But if your "Derby" shepherd and shepherdess are wearing the wrong shade of turquoise, they're fakes. Easier than that, however, is to look at the quality of the modeling and the fineness of the painting. "Slapdash" wasn't in the eighteenth-century vocabulary.

Where can I go to find eighteenth-century figures?
You're not very likely to find them at flea markets, or even at many local antiques shows. You will find them at New York auction houses, however. You'll see lots of copies, usually with faked marks, elsewhere. If you find an eighteenth-century mark on an eighteenth-century-type figure, assume it's not real.

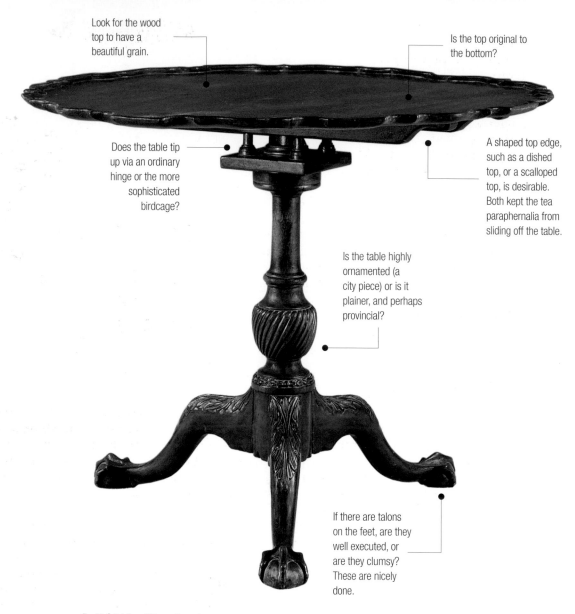

Look for the wood top to have a beautiful grain.

Is the top original to the bottom?

Does the table tip up via an ordinary hinge or the more sophisticated birdcage?

A shaped top edge, such as a dished top, or a scalloped top, is desirable. Both kept the tea paraphernalia from sliding off the table.

Is the table highly ornamented (a city piece) or is it plainer, and perhaps provincial?

If there are talons on the feet, are they well executed, or are they clumsy? These are nicely done.

A Little Backstory

Tea, by the eighteenth century, was an established social ritual, and one that involved all sorts of satisfyingly show-offy things: silver tea services, silver trays, porcelain cups and saucers, silver sugar tongs, tea strainers, and more. Among the most necessary accessories was the tea table, a tripod base with a round top that frequently had a mechanism (a "birdcage") underneath that allowed it to be tipped up and put against a wall when not in use. England, of course, is the motherland of afternoon tea.

Q & A

What exactly does the "birdcage" do?

The birdcage—called that because with pillars set between top and bottom blocks, it looks (something) like a birdcage—is a refinement. Primarily, it allows the table to tip upright and perhaps be pushed against a wall (thus saving space) or to become a useful fire screen (saving delicate skin). Some types of birdcages enable tabletops to revolve; some make the tops removable.

Why do there seem to be so many tea tables, old and new?

They are real classics. They're useful, they're pretty, they're versatile. Other furniture—the recamier couch, for instance, or the worktable with the sewing bag hanging beneath—were simply fads. Once women gave up lolling and got sewing machines, tables used specifically for tea couldn't last. But the shape and portability of the tripod table made it useful, especially for lamps today.

How do I tell the difference between an English tea table and those from other countries? And why would I care if it's English?

It isn't always easy, because the American version imitated the English version and both favored mahogany. On the whole, the English model may be a little fancier, and even decorated with inlay, while American examples used the birdcage more often. English furniture is much more susceptible to woodworm, as well.

As to your second question, well, we do only think in terms of "English" and "American" furniture, but Ireland, Sweden, Italy, and other countries on the Continent used tripod tables as well. Since the 1880s and the robber baron era, English furniture was It for Americans. Today, not so much!

Look For

- Unusual legs
- Carving on the knees, the baluster (that columnar support) and fancy feet
- A one-board top
- A dished top
- A gallery (that little latticework around the circumference of the circle)

Stay Away From

- A mismatched top and bottom
- Refinishing of any kind
- Later carving (usually shallower and less detailed than original carving)
- Legs that have been replaced or irreversibly repaired

Good This late eighteenth-century English mahogany tilt-top tea table has a resurfaced top that the auction house thinks may or may not be original to this base. It also has assorted repairs and has been refinished, although the English don't mind that as much as Americans do. It sold for only $700, which seems a decent price for a useful lamp table.

Better Here's a pretty eighteenth-century example with a scalloped, piecrust top. The legs, with their ball and claw foot, are in nice proportion to the size and style of the top—not too thick and decoratively carved. Combine that with the fact that it's awfully shiny (finish problems?) and the fact that English furniture is sort of "out" here, currently, and you have an attractive, period table for only $1,700.

Best This is a really unusual mahogany table, not just because its top is lobed and molded, and its legs are molded into scrolls, but because it has a fabulous provenance: It was owned by the celebrated British artist Dante Gabriel Rossetti, who bought it in the 1860s in a secondhand shop, where, he wrote, "Many a Chippendale chair or table could be met with and bought for next to nothing." Estimated to sell for around $20,000 to $30,000, its beauty and glamorous history caused it to sell for approximately $125,000.

Rose Medallion Punch Bowls

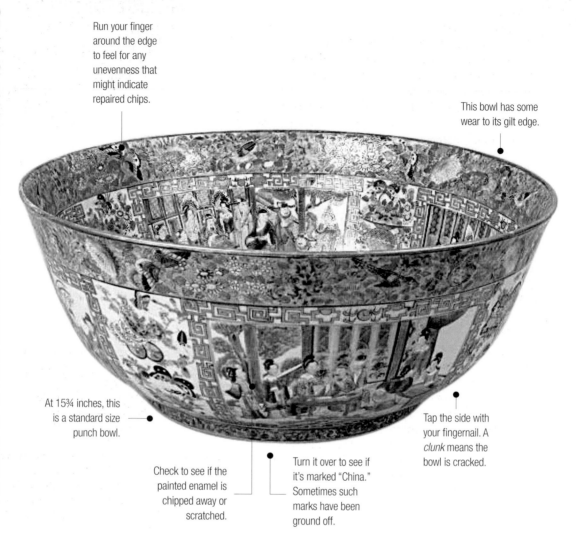

Run your finger around the edge to feel for any unevenness that might indicate repaired chips.

This bowl has some wear to its gilt edge.

At 15¾ inches, this is a standard size punch bowl.

Check to see if the painted enamel is chipped away or scratched.

Turn it over to see if it's marked "China." Sometimes such marks have been ground off.

Tap the side with your fingernail. A *clunk* means the bowl is cracked.

A Little Backstory

It certainly seems that from the eighteenth century on, our ancestors drank endless cups of punch. What else could account for the thousands upon thousands of rose medallion (that is, famille rose) punch bowls that today decorate our console tables, hold our most ambitious flower arrangements, and most often, provide a handy receptacle for storing our house and car keys.

Q & A

What exactly is famille rose?
The term is French for "pink family," and refers to the predominant color of the decoration on this type of Chinese porcelain. Early polychrome porcelains (those painted in several colors), might be famille verte (predominantly green), famille jaune (yellow) and more rarely, famille noire (black). But with the 1720 discovery of an opaque pink enamel, every European family that could afford it ordered huge sets of famille rose porcelain from China. It follows that most of what we see in America and Europe was made specifically for export.

In other words, it was a status thing to own?
It was, and in a way, it still is. The great families sometimes had their own crests incorporated into otherwise wholly Asian designs on plates and bowls, or in the latter part of the eighteenth century, sent their own European designs to be copied in famille rose colors. These are rare and collectible today. The original designs, however, with their reserves of Chinese scenes and landscapes, are always popular, although most of what we see was made in the nineteenth century.

Seriously, why do you suppose they had so many punch bowls?
When travel was more difficult and took considerably longer than it does today, people's house guests stayed longer, especially in the country, and this not infrequent overflow of distant family and friends often occasioned a ball. Punch—if you recall your Austen and Dickens—was the beverage of choice.

Look For
- Famille rose tableware depicting European subjects
- Armorial pieces (those with prominent coats of arms)
- Any American motif, usually flags or eagles
- Topographical scenes relating to the Western trade with China

Stay Away From
- Ordinarily, I would say chipped and cracked pieces, but if a piece is particularly early or special, collectors will nevertheless be interested.
- Chipped or cracked late-nineteenth- and certainly twentieth-century famille rose, because there's a great deal of it and it's still fairly easy to find a piece in good condition
- Careless painting, often the sign of a reproduction. Even though his work was only for export, the Chinese porcelain painter turned out moderately careful work.

Good The colors of this 14-inch diameter bowl, particularly when compared with those of the "Better" bowl, seem particularly harsh and unsubtle. Such bowls are often marked "Made in China," as is this one, an indication that they were certainly manufactured after 1892. You'll find them lighter in weight than the older wares. This example brought $118.

Better Unmarked, as is most genuine export porcelain, this 15¾-inch punch bowl brought $1,035 and depicts the usual scenes of courtiers, butterflies, and flowers rendered, by their anonymous painter, in the most lackluster fashion. The presence or absence of a stand (this is a fairly modern example, if not actually brand new) makes little difference to the selling price.

Best Except for its painted design, this circa 1785 bowl seems not very different from the "good" and the "better." It's that *design* that accounts for its $52,700 selling price. Around the circumference, depicted in traditional famille rose hues, are the business markets for foreigners in Canton: the Hongs. Although this was a popular decoration in the last quarter or so of the eighteenth century, it's seldom found on so large and perfect a bowl.

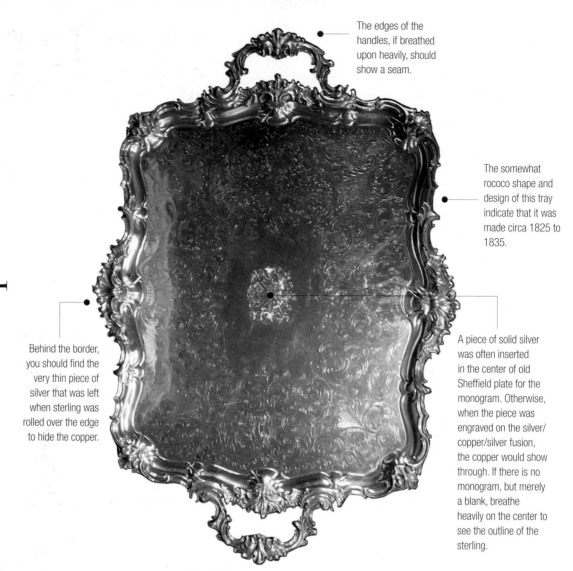

Antique Silver Plate

The edges of the handles, if breathed upon heavily, should show a seam.

The somewhat rococo shape and design of this tray indicate that it was made circa 1825 to 1835.

Behind the border, you should find the very thin piece of silver that was left when sterling was rolled over the edge to hide the copper.

A piece of solid silver was often inserted in the center of old Sheffield plate for the monogram. Otherwise, when the piece was engraved on the silver/copper/silver fusion, the copper would show through. If there is no monogram, but merely a blank, breathe heavily on the center to see the outline of the sterling.

A Little Backstory

In the days when not everyone could afford sterling silver, two basic types of silver plate—a cheaper silver look-alike—were developed: the sterling silver, copper, sterling silver "sandwich" that was first devised in the eighteenth century and electroplate, which was cheaper and faster to make and when done on a white-colored metal base was fairly convincing because the plated pieces usually imitated the shapes and designs of sterling silver. The older plated wares (known as Sheffield plate) are better quality than their descendants, but today it's the electroplated twentieth-century designs that excite collectors (when there are collectors!)

Q & A

How do I tell silver plate from silver?
On antique pieces, look for seams on handles, for a single small hallmark (in the shape of a bell, perhaps, or a hand), and a fine silver "wire" running just beneath the edges. This is the rolled-over silver that hides the copper in the sandwich. On modern silver plate, an EPNS on the bottom is always a giveaway (it stands for electroplated nickel silver) or simply the words "silver plate." Both old and new plated wares tarnish to a kind of iridescent gunmetal (sterling doesn't tarnish that way), and on either, the base metal can show through on worn high spots.

Why does so much silver plate seem to have hallmarks? It's confusing.
Mainly because sterling silver was hallmarked, and silver plate makers hoped to borrow some of that credibility (and confuse you). In England, early Sheffield plate manufacturers weren't allowed to imitate silver's four hallmarks, so those makers used a single identifying stamp, although much fine old plate has no marks at all. Later, they put a plethora of marks on the back that looked something like hallmarks—but not quite—and increased the possibility that a buyer would think he or she had purchased the real thing.

Does country of origin matter in silver plate?
Because it was invented and first flourished in England, most collectors of silver plate look for English wares. Tiffany and Gorham in the United States both manufactured plated silver, but it's not much sought after. Other countries' work in silver plate is interesting only insofar as the designs are attractive and popular.

Look For
- Small, single maker's marks
- High-style twentieth-century pieces
- Cocktail shakers from the 1920s, 1930s, and 1940s
- Old Christofle and Odiot plate, both French

Stay Away From
- Overpolished pieces
- Replated pieces. Silver plate loses all its collectible value when it's replated.
- Pieces that have been wrapped with rubber bands or plastic wrap, both of which leave ineradicable marks
- Tea sets, the dodo birds of silver plate
- Monogrammed plate (unless the monogram is your own)

Good It isn't just that the silver is worn through to the copper; it isn't just the fact that the repoussé (the relief work) is crudely executed on this five-piece set; it's mainly the fact that this is a *tea set* that caused it to sell for a mere $80. Who has guests to tea anymore?

Better These 20-inch convertible candelabra (the arms are removable, leaving a pair of candlesticks), are only late nineteenth century, though their design is much older. Three arms are repaired, as well, but they still brought $1,100. Who doesn't like a candlelit dinner table? (And you can't buy sterling for that.)

Best This silvered-bronze electroplated centerpiece and candleabra by the French firm Odiot is about as important as silver plate gets. Its modeler and chaser are known, as is the name of the mogul for whom it was made. It was also exhibited in the 1867 World Exhibition in Paris. And these account for its $120,000 selling price.

Teddy Bears

Feel for the Steiff button in the ear.

Check nose, mouth, and claws for hand stitching.

A pronounced nose and a hump are important features of the vintage Steiff bear.

Mohair "fur" is key, and certain colors are particularly rare.

Check for wear. A certain amount is acceptable.

Pads should be made of felt if the bear was manufactured before the 1930s.

A Little Backstory

Steiff teddy bears were first made in Germany in 1902, so today's collectible bears actually have their own literal "back" story: a hump. All Steiff teddies from before 1930 have a characteristic humped back because they were modeled on the real thing: the bears you see on *Nature*. Unlike the *Nature* bears, the Steiff bears also have an identifying button in their ear, though neither type became adorable until fairly recently.

Q & A

What was the button for?

Essentially, it is the company label. In 1904, an elephant trademark was used on the button, though from 1906 forward, the button read "Steiff." Because it was firmly fixed in the ear, it's not uncommon to find hundred-year-old bears with that original button still in place.

Let's say the button was lost, though. How else could I identify a valuable Steiff bear?

Its longish arms curve inward, as do its legs. Its close-set, black eyes were made of shoe buttons before World War I, and after that, black glass. Each bear has a somewhat conical muzzle and, of course, that hump.

Are there fakes?

Some bears have become so valuable (an extralarge example recently sold in England for almost $35,000!) that there are fakes, indeed. Check for uneven, clumsily stitched seams, and noses that have been insufficiently kissed.

Look For

- Bears with light mohair fur, and black bears, of which relatively few were made because they were frightening to toddlers
- Bears made of wool mohair
- Felt paw pads, which are older than velvet, leather, and, of course, plastic
- Cinnamon-color bears and white bears are highly sought after, but among the rarest is the Dicky bear, with its printed paw pads
- Hot-water bottle Steiff bears and bear-shaped purses
- Bears with movable metal-rod joints

Stay Away From

- Bears that are too perfect. They may be reproductions.
- Anything synthetic on the bear—from eyes to paws
- Bears with short arms and noses that aren't snoutlike. After the 1950s, these became common.
- Moth-eaten or truly threadbare bears—unless they're great rarities

Good A 9¼-inch Steiff mohair bear from the 1950s has a swivel head, jointed limbs, and an ear button. He also has two smaller friends who don't mind that the hair on the top of his head is thinning and that he's a little faded. These particular three little bears sold for $285.

Better A 16-inch tall, circa 1910 pale gold mohair teddy has all the right stuff: that splendid color, shoe-button eyes, a hand-sewn nose, an inverted Y mouth, beige felt pads, and the requisite button in the ear. He had some body and snout wear, but was still something of a buy at $4,800.

Best One of the very rare 45-inch-tall apricot bears, this circa 1906 model, as big as a child, has a center seam (initially, every seventh Steiff bear had a center seam in order to conserve fabric), shoe button eyes (made of gutta percha), cone-shaped nose, swivel joints, and, of course, an ear button. Despite having various bald spots, split and repaired ankles, and staining to his foot pads, he brought an astounding $35,800.

American Longcase Clocks

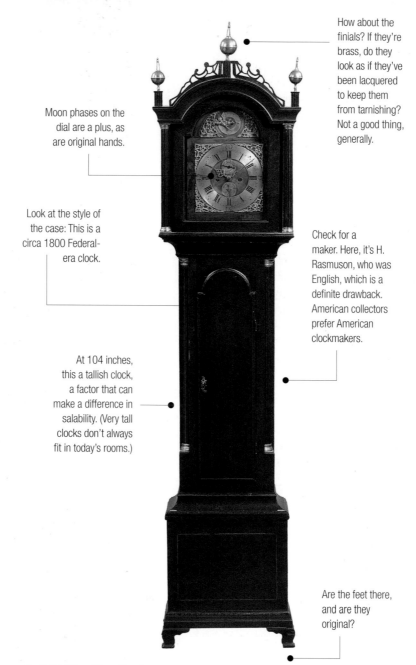

How about the finials? If they're brass, do they look as if they've been lacquered to keep them from tarnishing? Not a good thing, generally.

Moon phases on the dial are a plus, as are original hands.

Look at the style of the case: This is a circa 1800 Federal-era clock.

Check for a maker. Here, it's H. Rasmuson, who was English, which is a definite drawback. American collectors prefer American clockmakers.

At 104 inches, this a tallish clock, a factor that can make a difference in salability. (Very tall clocks don't always fit in today's rooms.)

Are the feet there, and are they original?

A Little Backstory

We think of them as grandfather clocks, but technically, they're longcase clocks. In the United States, the best ones were made predominantly in Pennsylvania, Massachusetts, and Connecticut, and many of the oldest American models had wooden faces and movements because brass was scarce.

Q & A

Do wooden movements keep good time?

When they were new, they did a decent job of it. But because wood warps and shrinks as it ages, old wooden works can't be depended on to be accurate timekeepers. Probably because of that, people replaced those wooden originals with later-made brass movements. This is why it's rare (and desirable) today, to find an American clock with its original wooden movement.

How can I tell if a longcase clock is American, and not, say, English or Scotch? They all look pretty much alike.

You can look on the face for the name and location of the maker, but if it isn't a well-known maker, such as one of the Willard family or Joshua Wilder of Massachussetts, determining the country of manufacture can be confusing. (For instance, Portsmouth and Epping are both American and English place-names.) So look at the materials and style of the case. The back panel should be pine and the carved scrollwork decorating the hood (if there is any scrollwork) might have those purely American "whale's tails," which look like . . . whale's tails.

Look For

- Beautiful proportions: hood to trunk to base
- Movements that are original to the cases they're in
- Original finials, which are in proportion to the case, and suitable to the era and the ornamental details of the case
- Movements by well-known makers
- Very tall clocks (if they fit your space) can be a bargain. Many homes today can only accept an eight-foot clock.
- American eagles, or any distinctly American decoration
- Makers' labels, inside the door or at the back

Stay Away From

- Replaced feet
- Missing or replaced finials or fretwork
- Plugged old holes in the dial; these can indicate a replaced face
- Missing feet—clocks were often cut down to allow them to fit in low-ceilinged rooms
- Replaced movements

Good With losses and chips to its wooden works, this early nineteenth-century clock by an unidentified maker might have some trouble keeping time. Replaced finials and extensive cracks and chips to the case help explain why it sold for only $850.

Better Retailed around 1900 by Theodore Starr in New York, this mahogany clock has shells and cherubim, scrolls and chimes. That date makes it late for serious clock collectors, however, and the style is not one that's currently popular among "furniture" collectors. Nevertheless, it brought $25,000 against a $30,000 to $50,000 estimate.

Best With an "Aaron Willard, Boston" inscription on its white enamel dial (also with moon phases and an American ship) as well as its original Aaron Willard label (engraved by Paul Revere) still inside the door, this perfectly proportioned and, somehow, chaste Federal era inlaid mahogany longcase clock is an Americana collector's dream. That's why it sold for $90,500.

Art Deco Jewelry

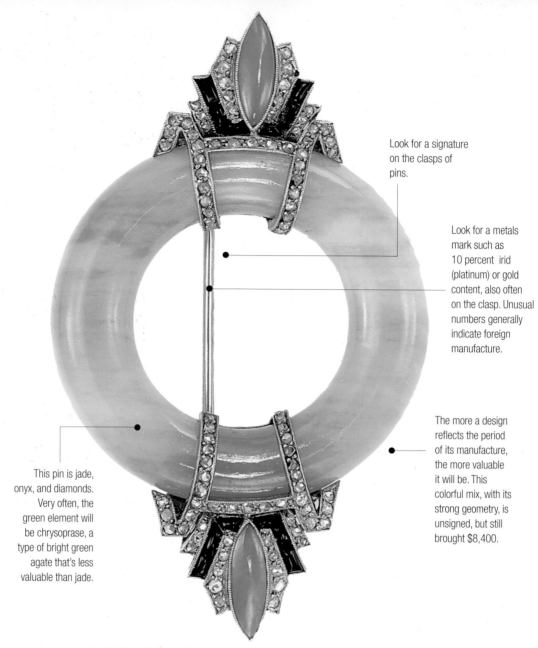

Look for a signature on the clasps of pins.

Look for a metals mark such as 10 percent irid (platinum) or gold content, also often on the clasp. Unusual numbers generally indicate foreign manufacture.

This pin is jade, onyx, and diamonds. Very often, the green element will be chrysoprase, a type of bright green agate that's less valuable than jade.

The more a design reflects the period of its manufacture, the more valuable it will be. This colorful mix, with its strong geometry, is unsigned, but still brought $8,400.

A Little Backstory

Jewelry of every century reflects fashion. Georgian jewelry is oval and delicate; Victorian jewelry is "busy"; and 1950s jewelry is all amoebas and boomerangs. Art Deco pieces—just like the doorways or flooring of the new skyscrapers—are geometric and often in combinations of green and black. They were sold in so many sizes and materials that from shopgirl to duchess, almost everyone could, and did, own a piece.

Q & A

What is it that makes a piece of jewelry expensive?
Intrinsic value. Stones have value. Metal settings—silver, gold, platinum—have value, while mahogany has no more intrinsic value than walnut, and art glass is not intrinsically more valuable than lead crystal. Stones and metal are valued for their weight. Thus a silver pin set with marcasite doesn't cost as much as a platinum pin with diamonds.

What is marcasite?
It's a name both for jewelry set with white iron pyrite that has been cut and faceted, polished, and set in metal—either silver or a base metal—and for the pyrite itself. Sometimes in this period, pieces of marcasite are mixed with colored stones and enamels. As in all twentieth-century arts, the work of some manufacturers has become collectible.

How do you tell marcasite from diamonds?
Aside from the fact that on close inspection marcasite is opaque. Interestingly, in Art Deco jewelry it's quite possible that some of the red and green colored stones mixed with the diamonds will be synthetic. Don't be fooled by a silver setting, though. Until jewelers began to utilize platinum, diamonds were frequently set in silver.

Look For
- Marcasite jewelry by Theodore Fahrner
- Marcasite jewelry marked "Made in Germany" or "Made in France"
- Pieces that have many of the Art Deco era's most desirable bells and whistles: spraying fountains, skyscrapers, slender (often nude) young women
- Pieces signed by one of the masters of Art Deco jewelry, especially by the French makers Cartier, Gérard Sandoz, Jean Desprès
- Imaginative designs

Stay Away From
- Obvious repairs. And look at the back to see if there are signs of a new clasp, for instance, or missing parts.
- Altered pieces—those earrings that were once cufflinks or that ring that is actually a pin soldered to a band
- Replaced stones, which will often be a different size, shape, or color
- Faked signatures—for example, Tiffany & Co. changed to Tiffany & Oc

Good This Art Deco brooch combines platinum, diamonds, and rubies and is typical of the ordinary jewelry of that era. Although all of its components are genuine, the design is a watered-down, commercial version of Art Deco style. This is the kind of pin that could be bought nationwide, in small jewelry stores. It recently brought a surprising $1,422 .

Better Essentially the same unexciting brooch, but this time, all in diamonds and mounted in platinum. It incorporates baguettes, very fashionable in the 1920s and 1930s, and at $1,900 it is, like the example above, a pleasant, somewhat common commercial piece, sold for a fair price.

Best It may seem surprising that such a singularly unpretentious carved emerald, ruby, and diamond pin could bring as much as $21,600, but its distinctively Art Deco design and use of stones, plus the desirable Mauboissin signature (one of the great Paris jewelers of the era) trumps every other consideration.

Nineteenth-Century English Porcelain Figures

Certain modelers and decorators—James Hadley at Worcester, for instance—are much sought after.

Animal groups are less common, and have a broad collector base.

Check both the back and the underside of the base for marks, but don't ever think of trusting them. Every detail—paste, palette, size, subject, and quality—must correspond with scholarly descriptions of the original.

Check fingers, toes, necks, and flora carefully for damage.

Look for tools or objects that might hint at the subject of the figure.

A Little Backstory

To tell the truth, the story of nineteenth-century English porcelain figures can probably be summed up in four words: eighteenth-century porcelain figures. Of course, much of the nineteenth century was given over to reproductions of the arts of preceding eras, and much of that was copied by machine. Yet you can't make or paint porcelain by machine, and thus, the big difference between the two centuries boils down to originality. And price. Later is cheaper!

Q & A

How do I tell the difference between the two?
One way is to refer to the palette charts that are available for eighteenth-century porcelains. If the flowers on a supposed Chelsea figure are painted sunshine yellow, rather than dirty yellow, it's nineteenth century. Another way is to look at the faces of the human figures. The Victorians did generic faces, usually "sweet." Eighteenth-century faces were generally not as pretty. They had a bit of character.

Will the usual nineteenth-century figure be soft-paste?
Not many were, because once the formula for bone china became known throughout England, around 1820, soft-paste was no longer used. (Some English "bone" china includes, along with the usual materials for porcelain, ashes of calcined bone, but other formulas include soapstone.)

Look For

- Flower encrustations on large pieces like vases
- English Derby, which was the main manufacturer of figures (and these were often copied in heavier earthenware by the numerous Staffordshire factories)
- Many factories—both English and European—sent their wares out of the factory to be painted. Some of these bear the signatures of the porcelain painting studios where they were decorated, although other studios bought blank white pieces and decorated them.
- A brilliantly colored ground (the main color of the plate or vessel), which usually indicates nineteenth-century manufacture
- Deep blues and more gold on figures

Stay Away From

- English copies of Meissen figures with forged crossed-sword marks
- Fine cracks in the body, which can either be firing cracks (present from inception) or damage cracks. Firing cracks, often wider and more random, are quite acceptable.
- Chips to delicate parts, such as flowers and fingers
- Poorly done repairs.

Good This unmarked 4½-inch putto, or cherub (the plural is putti), sold for $147. It's probably a copy of an eighteenth-century model, but given its apparently good condition and *almost* eighteenth-century coloration, that is a reasonable price.

Better With painted red anchor marks (placed there to make you think they're valuable, eighteenth-century Chelsea), these 9-inch nineteenth-century English figures are dressed in flowing draperies, another eighteenth-century conceit. The colors of their clothes and the surrounding flowers are harsher than the eighteenth-century originals would have been. This pair—and they often came as pairs—sold for $325.

Best Today, we think of Worcester as a single factory, but until comparatively recently, the city was home to many factories, one of which was Grainger, Lee & Co., the makers of this recumbent 4½-inch giraffe. The output of this firm was less formal than most other Worcester manufacturers, and it looked rather like Staffordshire. A rare choice for an English figure (being an animal seldom seen there, of course), this little giraffe brought $3,600.

Garden Seats

Ancient patterns are often copied on modern reproductions.

Sometimes there are genuine (or fake) reign marks painted in Chinese characters on the base. "Made in China," however, is always a guarantee of recent vintage. Sold for $1,659.

Garden seats with sealed bottoms often have pierced "handle" shapes and/or decorative emblems on their sides and tops. The original purpose of such openings was probably to allow hot gasses to escape during firing in the kiln.

The faux nailheads encircling barrel-shaped garden seats are called bosses and suggest actual kegs.

A Little Backstory

Chubby but ever-versatile, ceramic garden seats have been employed as footstools, pull-up tables (heavy ones), nicely waterproofed plant stands, and, yes, garden seats. When they aren't hiding under ferns, you'll find them in dressing rooms, family rooms, or sunning—in fat little flocks—around the pool. Endlessly adaptable and plump, garden seats may be the decorative equivalent of the Teletubbies.

Q & A

It seems I'm suddenly seeing these everywhere I look. Are they a fad?
Not unless you like your fads practically ancient. Garden seats are perennial. Since at least the seventeenth century they've been stock items in serene Chinese gardens, palmy Victorian conservatories, and twentieth-century living rooms.

Why do so many garden seats have Asian design features?
Because they first appeared in Ming-era China, the birthplace of porcelain. The very oldest were monochromes: all-over turquoise, perhaps, or green. By the nineteenth century, when they were being exported in huge numbers to Europe and England, they were painted to imitate elaborate and colorful cloisonné enamels. This was a European rather than a Chinese aesthetic, and resulted in all those familiar rose medallion patterns. From the 1870s until 1900 or so, factories in England, such as Minton and Wedgwood, produced popular garden seats in earthenware.

I know you can sit on them, but are they really comfortable?
Let's be honest. They're small and they're hard. They're also too low for our modern long legs. But three- to twelve-year-olds love them.

Look For

- Fine-quality painting. All Chinese examples are hand painted, and so are many Western ones. English makers, however, did some transfer printed seats toward the end of the nineteenth century.
- Interesting and unusual shapes. Elephants with little howdahs are ho-hum, but English majolica seats fashioned with—or even as—figures, birds, and animals are quite desirable.
- George Jones majolica garden seats have a shiny, viscous glaze, are highly detailed, brilliantly colored, and wildly collectible. They are marked "GJ," "GJ & Sons," and after 1873, the latter with a crescent.
- Minton garden seats, except for Secessionist wares (see below), are not generally as highly sought after as George Jones' wares.

Stay Away From

- A vivid and watery blue-green paint on "old" rose medallion wares. It's a dead giveaway.
- Carelessly painted copies of Chinese originals. Choose almost any modern reinterpretation over a sloppy imitation.
- Large unsightly chips. (Small chips can sometimes be painted out.)
- Cracks—especially if you plan on using the piece for seating. (On three- and four-hundred-year-old garden seats, cracks seem to be acceptable.)

Good This is the most basic of modern garden seats. Chinese in shape and general decoration, its coloration marks it as contemporary. If you turn it over, it may say "Made in China" on the bottom. At auction, it sells for about $25, but would cost more in a store.

Better This nineteenth-century Chinese garden seat shares the bosses (those little decorative buttons) and openwork on its top and sides with the "good" example, but has both age and an attractive famille rose and phoenix decoration to commend it. It brought $652.

Best While the most familiar garden seats are barrel shaped, many were made of majolica (a type of earthenware), particularly in England. This example is made by Minton in its Secessionist style, a very early twentieth-century artistic movement that in Minton's decoration, at least, took the form of brightly colored stylized flowers outlined by clay. Desirable today, this stamped "Minton" garden seat, with a date cipher for 1908, sold recently for $6,000.

Figured mahogany is attractive. Look for damage to the veneer. This table has some cracking veneer.

The lighter wood corner panels add interest to an otherwise conventional design. It sold for $1,840.

The heavy carving of the center post and legs indicates that it was manufactured late in the era, circa 1830.

Missing veneer can be easily repaired. If some is missing, check to see if it's thick or thin. Thick veneer is typical of genuine tables of this period.

A Little Backstory

Although America continued to copy French and English designs (Federal and Empire styles were, au fond, French), there were some very good craftsmen working here, among them the celebrated Duncan Phyfe, of New York. Phyfe actually *created* little early on. He simply adapted foreign designs to American taste. But very sophisticated furniture came from other American workshops, often with British-made casters and French bronze mounts, and card tables were a necessity in every home.

Q & A

What's the difference between Federal furniture and neoclassical furniture?
Actually, "Federal" describes an era in American history from approximately 1780 to 1830, while "neoclassical" is the style of furniture and architecture that was popular during that time. Until around 1810, American neoclassical furniture was influenced by English cabinetmakers Robert Adam and Thomas Sheraton. Thereafter, French taste held sway.

Then is it more or less the same as Regency furniture?
It is, but English pieces (and French), on the whole, are fancier, and since fashion arrived late to America, it started here later and ended later.

If English things are more sophisticated, why does American Federal furniture seem to be equally—or even more— expensive?
Americans are proud of their heritage. Inevitably, we are ready to pay more for our own art, our own history, than we pay for works from another country.

Look For

- Labeled pieces, either branded underneath, affixed with a glued-on paper label, or written in chalk or pencil in some hidden spot
- Verdigris (greenish) feet or supports; these were intended to resemble patinated bronze
- Hairy paw feet (exactly that), carved in wood
- Eagle-form elements
- Rosewood, which was more expensive than mahogany
- Fine carving

Stay Away From

- Late-nineteenth-century copies of Empire designs. These usually have clumsy or machined "carving."
- Pieces that are missing brass trim, or casters. Brass trim is costly to replace.
- Pieces on which stenciling has faded to ghostliness
- Circular saw marks on the underside, one mark of a reproduction
- Broken or replaced legs

Good A good example of the sort of copy that was popular at the *end* of the nineteenth century, this table has overlarge lion's paw feet with scalloped pompadours, shallow carving, and a clumsily rendered urn. From the center column to the shiny finish, it's a poor substitute for an original, and barely worth its $351 selling price.

Better This is a period table, circa.1825, but its maker has tried to do too much with the design. The combination of clustered columns as the center support with the incurving rosettes on the skimpy legs is too busy for the simply shaped rectangular top with its rounded corners. The lower edge has a brass band, and the stenciled gilding (intended to suggest gilt-bronze mounts) takes it altogether over the top. It sold for $3,500.

Best Combining gilding and verigris with carved cornucopia supports and hairy paw feet, this New York table is well designed, in good condition and brought a fair $10,000. One could only wish it were of rosewood veneer instead of mahogany.

Blankets

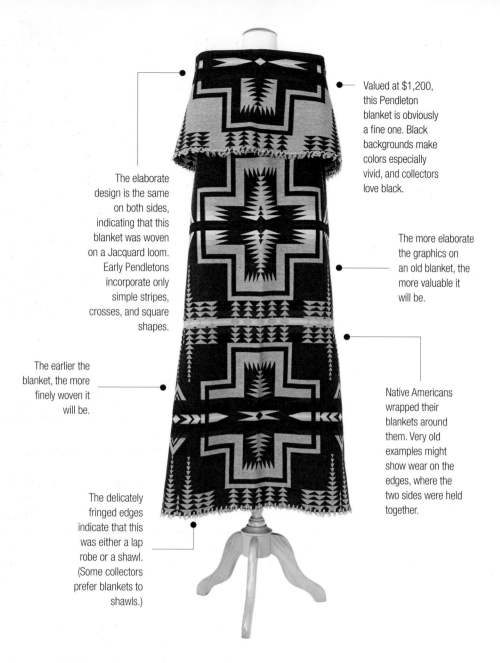

Valued at $1,200, this Pendleton blanket is obviously a fine one. Black backgrounds make colors especially vivid, and collectors love black.

The elaborate design is the same on both sides, indicating that this blanket was woven on a Jacquard loom. Early Pendletons incorporate only simple stripes, crosses, and square shapes.

The more elaborate the graphics on an old blanket, the more valuable it will be.

The earlier the blanket, the more finely woven it will be.

Native Americans wrapped their blankets around them. Very old examples might show wear on the edges, where the two sides were held together.

The delicately fringed edges indicate that this was either a lap robe or a shawl. (Some collectors prefer blankets to shawls.)

A Little Backstory

Cuddly and comforting and useful at picnics, a little too heavy now and then, but not heavy enough now and then, America's blankets—highly and suddenly collectible—are American history. From the blankets that cloaked Geronimo, to the blankets that cushion our bleachers, to the "blankies" beloved by our babies, we're devoted to our all-American blankets.

Good This is a recent example of a classic Hudson's Bay blanket, with no points on the edge. It's priced at $250, which is about what they sell for new.

Better With prime colors and so tightly woven and thick that it looks and feels like wool, this cotton Beacon, sometimes called a camp blanket, incorporates the ombré shading that's so costly to replicate today. This example is worth $450 to $550.

Best Priced at $950, with patterns based on Indian designs, the colors of this square-cornered Pendleton (c.1920s) are reminiscent of Adirondack summer camps. Though subtle and unusual, it's not as desirable as the blanket opposite.

Look For

- *Paper labels on Beacon blankets.* These were often victims of washing machines. If you find one (they were *big*), it adds to value.
- *Rounded corners.* Collectors look for the pre-1910 rounded corners on Pendleton blankets. After that date, corners are square.
- *Unusual patterns,* such as the 1937 Hudson's Bay Coronation blanket (deep blue with red stripes) or with Beacon, the pictorials

Stay Away From

- *Moth holes.* Hold the blanket up to the light to look for moth damage, though with really rare examples, damage is acceptable. (Before you add a new blanket to your collection, have it dry-cleaned first.)
- *Synthetic Beacon blankets.* All-cotton models made before 1945 are preferred. (Synthetics shine, by the way, and cotton doesn't.)
- *Stained, shrunken, or asymmetrical blankets and colors that have run.* Fringes are found mainly on lap robes or shawls.
- *Ugly color combinations.* Beauty is in the eye of the beholder, but orange, turquoise, and olive green? Well . . .

Q & A

How does something as everyday as blankets become collectible?
Although Americans began to rediscover Native American art and objects in the 1960s, today's desirable blankets aren't Native American at all. They just look it. They were first created to be *sold* to Native Americans, to be worn by them and used by them, so while they're only Native American by association, that, as well as their splendid patterns, makes them collectible.

I thought Native Americans wove their own blankets. Why would they buy them?
They *did* weave their own, that is, until blanket manufacturers, such as Hudson's Bay and Pendleton, began to offer machine made blankets at every far-flung trading post. The geometric designs of these "trade blankets" were traditional, as were their familiar colors, and their warmth was unparalleled. Such store-bought goods eventually came to replace the homemade for Native Americans, and those blankets evolved into a staple of our early commerce.

I once read that those little black stripes on Hudson's Bay wool blankets had meaning.
Old Hudson's Bay blankets, with their colorful stripes, were known as point blankets, because along one edge, short indigo stripes were woven into each to indicate size and weight. Worn by tribes throughout the United States, the blankets were actually woven in England. The point system (the one-point blanket, the lightest weave, weighed 3 pounds, 1 ounce and was 2 feet 8 inches wide by 8 feet long) did not indicate that each stripe meant the blankets were worth so many beaver pelts. It denoted the overall finished size.

Nineteenth- and Twentieth-Century European Dolls

Check the material the head is made from: This is celluloid, a twentieth-century material, which means the doll has to be from that century.

The maker's name (in this case, Jumeau, the nineteenth-century French manufacturer) is on the back of the head, under the hair.

Size counts. At 15 inches, this is a good-size doll.

Look for original clothes.

Its French regional costume marks this one as a souvenir doll.

Skinner, Auctioneers & Appraisers, Marlborough, MA $70.

A Little Backstory

The very best dolls were always the European dolls. Germany, especially, had a long history of toy making (Santa's surname, after all, is Claus) and end-of-the-nineteenth-century German dolls were among the most beautifully made and were highly sought after. Many German companies continued exporting their popular babies well into the twentieth century, until the beginning of the Second World War, when, for obvious reasons, their primacy and manufacturing capabilities ceased.

Q & A

"Babies"? Were there baby dolls?
Actual "baby" dolls weren't introduced until 1909. Before that, children played with "child" dolls, and even earlier, with "adult" dolls. Once little girls had their very own infants to mother, however, baby dolls became their universal first love, until—puzzlingly—the debut of Barbie in the 1960s.

How do I know whether I have a twentieth-century doll, and how can I tell who made it?
You can look at hairstyles and clothes, of course, or for less work and more fun, you can look at trademarks. By the twentieth century, these were placed on the back of the head under the wig or on the back of the shoulder plate. Many of the initials, names, and factory inventory numbers that you'll find have been traced, and can indicate the age of the doll.

I'll bet some manufacturers' dolls are more valuable than others.
Naturally! Though during the twentieth century, the supremacy of French and German dolls, with their carefully painted faces and well-made clothes, began to give way somewhat to twentieth-century parents' preferences (and they were the doll buyers, after all) for American-made. It wasn't a total coup, however, because Käthe Kruse's German dolls and Lenci dolls from Italy still competed in American toy stores with American-made dolls at FAO Schwarz. These two, along with other European dolls, are still desirable today.

Look For

- Original paint, especially on faces
- Dolls with Asian or black heads, and pre-World War II Native American dolls
- The proper number of fingers and toes
- An original wig, preferably with original hair set
- Bisque-head dolls with realistic facial expressions, such as delight, or more often, tears
- Dolls that were costly when new, which will still be costly today

Stay Away From

- Repainted faces
- Broken fingers and toes
- No wig or a replacement wig
- Signs of aging, such as discoloration and crazing in the material from which the doll was made

Good This early twentieth-century 15-inch bisque and cloth baby doll has "sleep" paperweight eyes that close when she's laid on her back (a late nineteenth-century innovation) and a cloth body with composition hands. Unfortunately, she's lost two fingers of her right hand, and all five fingers on her left. Condition is everything with twentieth-century dolls because so many are available to collectors, thus this well-loved baby brought a mere $50.

Better Made sometime between 1930 and 1952, this is a 14-inch Käthe Kruse–type doll named Johanniskind. While her clothes are original, her blouse is discolored; she's missing her shoes; her papier-mâché head has developed heavy crazing; and not only that, her washable muslin body has yellowed with age. Because these dolls are possibly *the* most desirable cloth dolls, however, she still brought $935.

Best At 22 inches, this is a largish doll, a 1914 JDK (Kestner) bisque Hilda baby. Her brown eyes are stationary with painted lashes, and she has her original body and wig, although the wig has been glued down so securely it can't be removed to expose the *full* set of markings beneath. She's wearing a cotton nightshirt and a diaper, so it couldn't have been her outfit that drove her price up to $2,070.

Scratches indicate wear.

Old examples have crisper details because they were cast in finer sand.

Watch out for lost or replaced bobeches (those removable candle cups).

Because overpolishing reduces value, handle fine old brass with gloves on.

Look out for *visible* old solder repairs on brass (this one is *in*visible), which diminish value.

Old models come apart—nozzle, shaft, foot—often with a design element to disguise the joint.

On early candlesticks, the underside of the base will have been skimmed on a lathe.

If the base is marked with the country of origin, manufacture is after 1890. Look for seams. They indicate age.

Brass was once expensive, and candlesticks were made hollow to save metal.

A Little Backstory

Yes, brass candlesticks are fairly useless, because with the exception of all women over forty and several million romantics, who really needs candlelight today? But in spite of their obsolescence—thank Edison—they're still being made. The vintage ones are nicer, though, and even nicer than those are the umpty-ump thousands of antique candlesticks that actually date from prelightbulb times. They're the ones with the romance built in.

Good Twisted stem candlesticks, such as this small Victorian example, came in several sizes, some fairly large. This fellow's brass shaft is awkwardly twisted and carelessly filed, and it's a single—worth $45.

Better Push-up sticks like these for $375 were common. Often made in Birmingham, the center of English brass. Nineteenth-century pairs are often uncleaned underneath.

Best After 250 years of polishing (which diminishes detail), but adds much romantic luster), these circa 1750 candlesticks are unusual and might have pseudosilver hallmarks. At $1,200 they're good quality.

Look For

- Interesting or unusual design elements such as twists, faceted shafts, or the natty little beading called pearl work
- Brass that is beautifully cast, chased, or engraved. The best of early craftsmen took their time.
- Manufacturers' marks on the base (never on American sticks, at least until circa 1850)
- Adjustable nozzles that accommodated any diameter candle, telescoping candlesticks, and for gadget buffs, any that have unique, often patented, mechanisms

Stay Away From

- Dented candlesticks
- The blurry, too-soft edges that indicate either modern manufacture or, equally bad overpolishing
- Pairs in which one is visibly imperfect
- Overtly religious decoration
- Old brass that's been lacquered (although it *is* removable)
- Late-nineteenth-century copies of earlier designs, which have now picked up enough age to be dangerous

Q & A

How can I tell if a brass candlestick is old? They all look old to me.
Early brass candlesticks were cast in three pieces: a base and the two halves of the shaft; so you should see seams where those two halves were joined. Also, until about 1890, the undersides of bases were neatly cleaned of the roughnesses left by the casting process. If the bottom looks dark and pebbly, as if the hot brass had been rubbed with a cloth, it's probably new.

Should I expect to pay more for brass candlesticks made in the era before electricity?
Considering that they were once necessities, candlesticks were surprisingly hard to make. The process included sand casting the molten metal, filing off the burrs, lathing the bottom, adding occasional embellishments, such as chasing or engraving, and finally, polishing. So yes, you'll pay more, because collectors value that craftsmanship, not to mention that lustrous patina.

Are there differences between English and American candlesticks, and how can I tell them apart?
It's not easy. Some English models have the maker's name impressed under the base (American models never do), and certain shapes, such as seventeenth-century trumpet-base candlesticks, are unique to England. But on the whole, both countries copied the same sterling silver shapes and used the same yellow metal alloy of copper and zinc. American candlesticks are more valuable here; the Brits prefer their own.

But I won't have to pay as much for brass as I would for silver, will I?
Surprisingly, materials aren't key. Age is. Condition being equal, a fine pair of early American brass candlesticks is usually pricier, for instance, than any commercially made sterling silver from the mid-twentieth century.

The concave top rail wrapped the shoulders. You could even throw an arm over it.

While we don't know whether the chairs painted on terra-cotta pots had central back splats (because someone's usually sitting in them), a chair back is stronger for having one.

An ebonized finish such as this one is not uncommon on klismos chairs.

The four saberlike legs are typical—the curvier, the better.

In antiquity, lacings of leather or fabric made sturdy, springy seats. On this chair from the 1930s, there appears to be a slip seat.

A Little Backstory

Although no one has ever *sat* on an original Greek klismos chair (that's KLIZ-mäs), because not one has actually survived, it's nevertheless The Chair. In use since the eighteenth century, when Pompeii and all things classical were resurrected, it's not a glam chair—not a throne by a long shot—(and not wildly comfortable either), but it is perennially beloved. From the moment we first spied it on Greek pots, the elegant klismos has been reproduced, reinvented, and refreshed. It's the most popular chair we've never seen.

Good This typical nineteenth-century American chair is made of handsome tiger maple, though it seems a shy little kind of klismos, a sort of country cousin. Despite some restorations, it sold for $375.

Better The buyer who paid $4,500 for this walnut chair by American designer T. H. Robsjohn-Gibbings presumably knew that it can be bought new today for $5,000.

Best These are Gustavian chairs, circa 1800. Four straight legs on klismos chairs—a Roman variation on the form—were not uncommon on Scandinavian neoclassical furniture. This antique pair brought $23,750.

Look For

- Labeled or signed examples, both antique and modern
- Sets of klismos chairs. They were often dining chairs.
- Chairs made circa 1800, which are frequently narrower than we're used to today. Luxury models were made of expensive woods, such as fine mahogany.
- Original, unretouched paint, originally used to disguise the cheaper woods
- Comfort. I suspect the Greek original wasn't easy on the back.

Stay Away From

- Chipped paint on vintage (twentieth century) chairs. Collectors tolerate it and even like it on antique chairs; but the newer the chair, the more perfect it's expected to be.
- Klutzy front legs (by which I mean almost any vertical leg)
- Klutzy rear legs
- Completely upholstered chairs, which are heavy and spoil the classic line
- Chairs with bad proportions, like too-short backs or stumpy saber legs

Q & A

What actually makes a chair a klismos chair?
Basically, it's the concave top rail that's curved to embrace the shoulders of the sitter, and those four incurved saber legs. Some chairs have vertical or horizontal back splats and some have none at all. (Because this element isn't usually visible in the Greek original, we don't quite know what's "right.") There are many variants with perfectly straight front legs too, but they tend to look clunky.

Are they only available in wood?
Until recently, the klismos form was primarily made of wood, although metal examples do exist. During the twentieth century the chair was manufactured in any new material that came along. Occasionally, you'll find an example that's fully upholstered, seat and back. We know, though, the 400 BC Greek chair was made of interwoven thongs and wasn't upholstered.

Am I better off looking for old chairs or new ones?
That's a good question. If the old example has beautiful proportions, is crafted of rich woods or of woods with splendid grain, is in good condition (that is, it's sit-on-able), and it's within your budget, buy it, certainly. And if a new one is by a known architect or designer, or if it's a witty riff on the ancient form, buy that. Either way, never "invest." Buy only what you love.

How do I recognize an old chair?
A few pointers: The tips of the legs will be smooth to the touch. (Legs with metal taps on the ends are usually modern.) If there's a fixed upholstered seat, there should be lots of nail holes to testify to its many reupholsterings. The chair will also have numerous dings and dents, all softened and worn by dusting and time.

The funky clock and pitched roof are additions. Purists might choose to remove them.

Made in the late nineteenth century, this three-story dollhouse, at almost 5 feet tall, is taller than most children.

This wooden box-back English dollhouse comes with chandeliers, tiny clocks, and dreadful paintings.

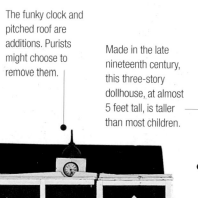

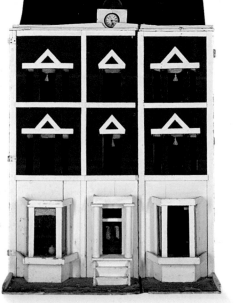

A staircase with oriental runners and furnished landings (there's even a birdcage) are luxurious extras.

A real plus for collectors, the house retains its original damask wallpapers, window blinds, bamboo mats, fireplaces, and kitchen shelves.

A Little Backstory

I'll bet you thought dollhouses were for little girls. But they started out as miniature rooms for grown-ups to furnish. In seventeenth-century Holland, in fact, one dollhouse fancier spent 20,000 to 30,000 guilders on her hobby, the cost of a real house at the time! Eventually, of course, children (and all right, some of their parents) co-opted them, because they realized that dollhouses could be painted, papered, carpeted, curtained, furnished, and wow—played with!

Good Here's a mid-twentieth-century tin dollhouse that even has a yard. Well, yes, part of the garage and a front portico are missing. And the chimney's askew. But there's probably $35 worth of fun here.

Better A new back-opening Princess Anne Victorian has uncharacteristically restrained architecture. (You can add two more rooms to its current six, or even a conservatory.) Completely put together with painted exterior and shingled roof, it's $695.

Best You won't find much medieval furniture for this vintage painted wooden castle, but with hidden stables beneath the floor, trap doors, hidden entrances, and (oooh!) boiling oil pipes who needs Gothic chairs? It brought $900.

Look For

- Vintage dollhouses with special features like real glass windows or interior doors
- Makers' marks, which are often underneath, on the foundation, or on the floor. (Though not all dollhouses were marked. You might have to track down the manufacturer's original catalogue for a picture.)
- Still-bright coloration
- The original box—a big plus
- A clean house (utterly self-explanatory)

Stay Away From

- Vintage houses with missing parts. For example, the 1920s Converse one-room bungalow was originally offered with detachable front steps. You don't want that house without those steps.
- Nonoriginal elements. If they've added a chimney and repainted or changed the roofline of a vintage dollhouse, its value is diminished.
- Everything you'd object to in a *real* house: cracked or warped wood, peeling paint, buckled wallboard and rust. Not to mention wet basements.

Q & A

I've seen some dollhouses that dwarf my children. Is bigger better?
Bigger is inevitably more expensive, but it's only better if you actually have room for a 4- or 5 foot tall dollhouse. Lots of twentieth-century dollhouses come in several sizes, though, so if you're not ready for The Estate model, you can have a small estate as a starter house. There are bungalows too.

Dollhouse people talk about "play scale." What is that?
Modern American dollhouses (and "modern," in this context doesn't mean Frank Gehry) are scaled so that 1 inch equals 12 inches. Barbie dollhouses are scaled for Barbies, and are bigger: 1 inch equals 6 inches. Antique dollhouses generally predate such classifications.

And what is "play worn"?
Play worn is toy-dealer-speak for "Don't spend money on a this toy unless it's really rare." Of course, eighteenth- or nineteenth-century dollhouses and their furnishings are worn, most often, and collectors accept that. But the nearer we get to the present, the more they demand perfection. That's why the best old dollhouse of all, sadly, is the one that's never been played with.

Where's the best place to find a vintage dollhouse?
For "vintage," the most obvious answer is the Internet. But if you like to touch before you buy, both old and new models can be seen and touched in the booths of the hundreds of miniature dealers who exhibit at shows or at big toy stores. The beautiful part about nonvirtual shopping is that you can learn from the experts.

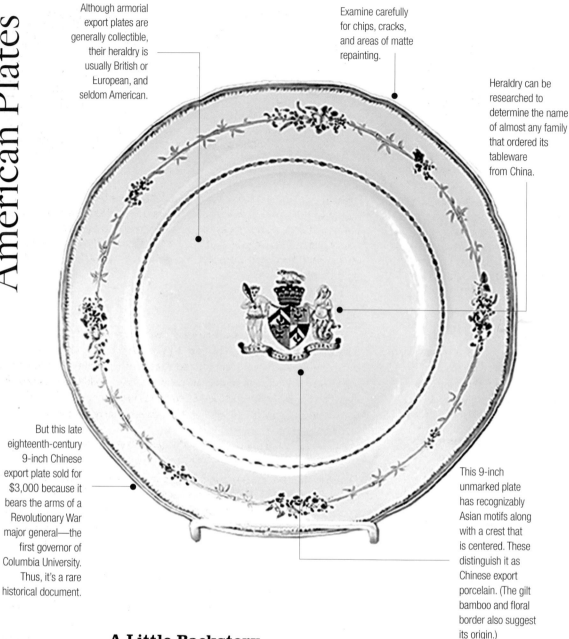

Although armorial export plates are generally collectible, their heraldry is usually British or European, and seldom American.

Examine carefully for chips, cracks, and areas of matte repainting.

Heraldry can be researched to determine the name of almost any family that ordered its tableware from China.

But this late eighteenth-century 9-inch Chinese export plate sold for $3,000 because it bears the arms of a Revolutionary War major general—the first governor of Columbia University. Thus, it's a rare historical document.

This 9-inch unmarked plate has recognizably Asian motifs along with a crest that is centered. These distinguish it as Chinese export porcelain. (The gilt bamboo and floral border also suggest its origin.)

A Little Backstory

Even though it's Limoges, that tableware you inherited from your aunt Judy—those dozens of 22K gold-rimmed plates, cups, soups, bread and butters—aren't really valuable. (Except to you, of course). It might surprise you to know, however, that there are plates   individual plates—that are interesting from a historical point of view. And surprisingly collectible.

Good This curious little 6-inch plate is transfer printed with a cartoon of a clambake taking place in a clamshell surrounded by Indians. The unusual subject, and a legend referring specifically to Fort Townsend, Washington, account for its $140 selling price.

Better On a 10-inch pearlware plate dating from 1830, a very grand American eagle beneath thirteen stars. Despite the two small rim chips and some minor surface crackle, its age and all-American subject drove the price to $1,700.

Best The eagle on this 9³⁄₈-inch printed and hand-painted plate immediately makes it collectible. But it's from the Royal Purple service used by the Lincolns in the White House, and that makes it worth $27,600.

Look For

- American eagles
- Plates that have the artist's signature or monogram on the back
- Plates retailed by Tiffany & Co.
- Serving plates with or by all of the above (as opposed to dinner plates)

Stay Away From

- Cracks. Rest the plate on its rim, and *ping* it with your fingernail—a dull thunk should send you looking for a crack or repair.
- Chips (except on particularly rare plates). Chips on the back of a plate are often acceptable.
- Badly worn gilding
- A faded (oh, those dishwashers!) or a scratched central image

Q & A

I always thought Limoges was a top name in china. Are you saying that it isn't?
Limoges, a French porcelain, enjoyed great status in America in the nineteenth century, and it continued almost to the present day. The company may have cemented its reputation here when Mary Todd Lincoln chose it for the White House. Currently, however, there's just not much of a market for secondhand porcelain tablewares—even those made by Limoges.

But what about hand painting, and other great names, such as Royal Crown Derby and Royal Worcester and Wedgwood?
Hand painting was the preferred way to decorate china until transfer printing—cheaper and faster—was developed. And while it's certainly a more costly process these days, for centuries it was also the only way. The good old firms are still good, and old, but the fact is, people don't entertain the way they used to, and it seems that "good china" is less and less a prerequisite of modern entertaining.

Then how is it that one plate can be valuable?
A plate known to have been painted by a listed American artist, for instance, will have unusual value, as will Chinese export plates from the eighteenth and nineteenth centuries that were decorated particularly for the American market. (You can spot those flags and eagles.) And if a plate is of American interest—either artistically or historically—some American will want to own it.

How do I recognize Chinese export porcelain?
Once you've seen it, it's hard to mistake it for Western-made porcelain. To begin with, it's almost always unmarked. Nineteenth-century examples, particularly, are often heavier and coarser than European wares made at the same time. It helps to know that the Chinese saved their best work for themselves.

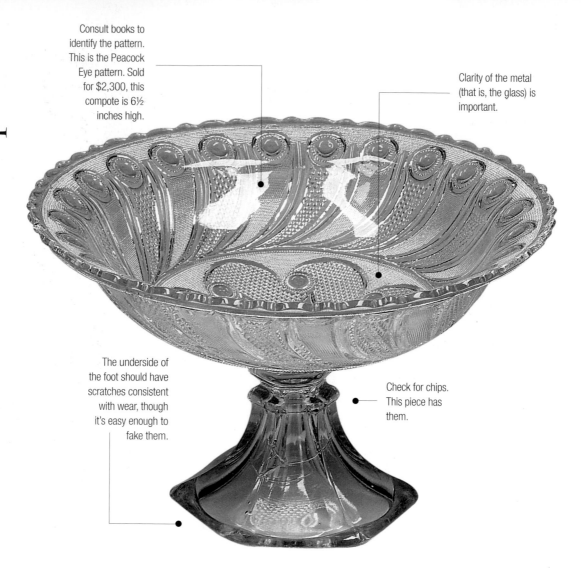

Clear Glass Compotes

Consult books to identify the pattern. This is the Peacock Eye pattern. Sold for $2,300, this compote is 6½ inches high.

Clarity of the metal (that is, the glass) is important.

The underside of the foot should have scratches consistent with wear, though it's easy enough to fake them.

Check for chips. This piece has them.

A Little Backstory

Even though it was mass-produced, blown and pressed American glass has been collected for decades, while its popularity has waxed and waned. (Dainty cup plates were a passion in the 1940s, for instance, but where are they now?) The comparatively inexpensive and lacy Sandwich glass was so well liked that it was exported to the Caribbean and South America. Glass shapes, however, of the type seen in these compotes, were often modeled on the shapes of silver, a far more costly tableware.

Q & A

How does one even begin to tell one type of glass from another?
Pressed glass differs from mold-blown glass in that it has
a smooth interior and visible exterior mold lines. Mouth-
blown glass is seamless.

But how do any of those differ from cut glass?
Cut glass has always been a more expensive product to
make because every facet, at least until recently, was hand
ground. It used to be sharp to the touch, as opposed to
pressed glass, which merely feels rough.

Should I expect to find makers' names on compotes?
Signatures and labels aren't typical of early nineteenth-
century glass, and anyway, our dependence on them—in
my opinion—is a dubious modern convenience, an attempt
to make collecting "easy." Before you believe in any
signature on *any* type of art—and that includes paintings—
make a checklist of everything you know about what it
ought to be, what it should have on it, and what it ought to
look like. Smarts and research trump labels.

Look For

- Blue and purple Sandwich glass. They're both very rare, as are
  all Sandwich's dark colors.
- Important pieces, such as vases and centerpieces—and
  compotes—tend to be more valuable than smaller tableware.
- Unusual shapes
- Seldom-seen patterns, particularly in Sandwich glass
- American early nineteenth-century blown glass

Stay Away From

- Reproductions of Sandwich glass, most of which was made for
  the twentieth-century market
- Buying vintage "gift shoppe" glass (*and* gift shoppes)
- Modern pressed glass, which is often lighter in weight than the
  original
- Continental pressed glass, which is very well made and can look
  American. But if the pressed design can be felt on the inside, for
  instance, the piece might be French.
- Toothpick holders, which appeared very late in the nineteenth
  century. The use of those contents may have been (and still is)
  considered uncouth.

Good The auctioneer thought this 14-inch-high pressed glass
frosted compote was nineteenth century. And if that is true and it
isn't a reproduction, then someone got a real bargain. Okay, the
dog's ear is a little chipped, and there's a bubble in the glass of the
base, but wow, $25?

Better A good example of a colorless blown-glass compote,
this 10-inch-high example has attractive proportions, and its ribbed
bowl is very much like the nineteenth-century glass manufactured
in New Jersey. Evidently, more than one bidder thought so,
because it outstripped its estimate of $300 to $400 to bring $850.

Best Its splendid yellow color aside, this is the genuine
Sandwich glass. It's that color combined with its Princess Feather
and Baskets of Flowers pattern that caused this small, 6-inch-high
compote to bring $42,000.

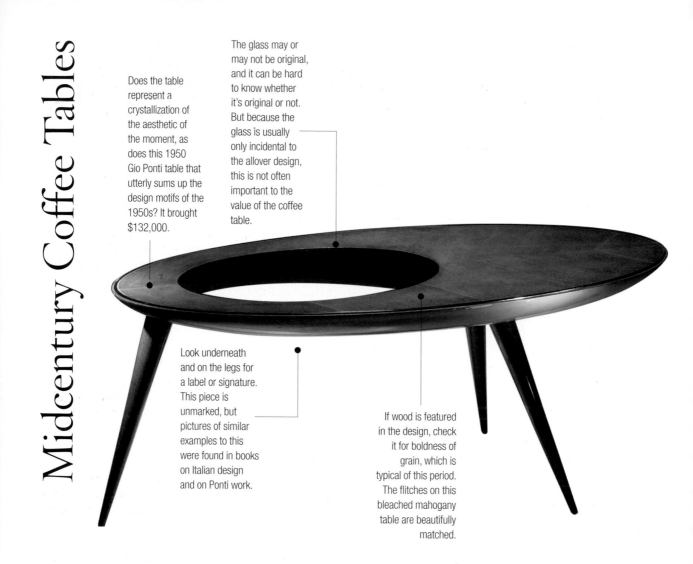

Does the table represent a crystallization of the aesthetic of the moment, as does this 1950 Gio Ponti table that utterly sums up the design motifs of the 1950s? It brought $132,000.

The glass may or may not be original, and it can be hard to know whether it's original or not. But because the glass is usually only incidental to the allover design, this is not often important to the value of the coffee table.

Look underneath and on the legs for a label or signature. This piece is unmarked, but pictures of similar examples to this were found in books on Italian design and on Ponti work.

If wood is featured in the design, check it for boldness of grain, which is typical of this period. The flitches on this bleached mahogany table are beautifully matched.

A Little Backstory

Despite the fact that is has Middle Eastern antecedents, the 18-inch-high coffee table is pretty much a twentieth-century piece of furniture. Not only was it an entirely new idea (rather like the ladies' worktable was in the eighteenth century and the center table was in the nineteenth century), it also lent itself to being made in any number of fabulous new materials. All by itself, then, the coffee table is capable of summing up every advance in twentieth-century design. Perhaps that explains why it can be among the most costly types of twentieth-century furniture.

Good

(Note: All these tables sold for remarkable prices. They demonstrate the current muscular state of the midcentury market.) A 59-inch-long acrylic waterfall by Charles Hollis Jones, known for his work in acrylic sheet, sold for $11,400.

Better Like his well-known "rudder" dining table, this 50 x 36-inch Isamu Noguchi coffee table for Herman Miller has two aluminum legs, both stamped "Alcoa," and one leg of birch (the birch dates it to around 1950). This table has had only one owner since it was made, and it sold for $66,000.

Best A 1954, 35½-inch Gio Ponti table from Diamond House in Venezuela (among the architect's most important commissions) is made of enameled steel and brass with a glass top and it sold for a dazzling $156,000.

Look For

- Shapes that bespeak the period in which they were made. Boomerangs or amoebic shapes scream 1950s, while waterfall tables are pure 1960s.
- Anything that seems to experiment with new materials, or with new ways of working with old materials
- Labels or signatures
- Prototypes (that is, pieces that were templates for furniture that may (or may not) have been put into production). These are one of a kind.
- Early catalogues and advertisements, which can help you identify designers, manufacturers, and prototypes

Stay Away From

- Overused, diluted, or too commercial designs
- Water stains and cigarette burns on wood tops
- Overly scratched glass or plastic table tops
- Nonfunctional shapes. Your table should be expected, after all, to comfortably hold at least one canapé tray and two drinks.

Q & A

Are some materials used in coffee tables especially valuable?
Not really. Plastic tables can bring more than wooden tables, and bronze can bring less than both. Rather like the fascination with labeled handbags and shoes, this is a field that is all about designers. But unlike handbags and shoes, your coffee table won't wear out.

What about reproductions?
While reproductions will certainly hold as many magazines, ornaments, cocktails, and "coffee table books," they're simply not original art. In contrast, when you buy a table actually made by a Nakashima or a Giacometti, you're buying three-dimensional, functional art.

But that kind of thing is hugely expensive. Couldn't I do as well with a Victorian table, say, with its legs cut to coffee table height?
Besides wreaking irreparable harm on a piece of antique furniture (although there are those who think Victorian furniture deserves even worse), you'll have a travesty: a table with obviously cut-down legs.

Here and there I see mentions of "prototypes," and these seem to be amazingly costly. How do I know if a piece is a prototype?
The scholarship for twentieth-century furniture is far from complete, so if you suspect such a thing, you may have to do quite a lot of research yourself. If you're looking at a table that's well crafted of costly materials, for instance, and you know the midcentury coffee table field well enough to know that this is something rare (not just something *you've* never seen before), hit the books or the Internet. Ask knowledgeable dealers and scour early catalogues, magazine ads, and photos. Sometimes factory records are useful too.

Figural Napkin Holders

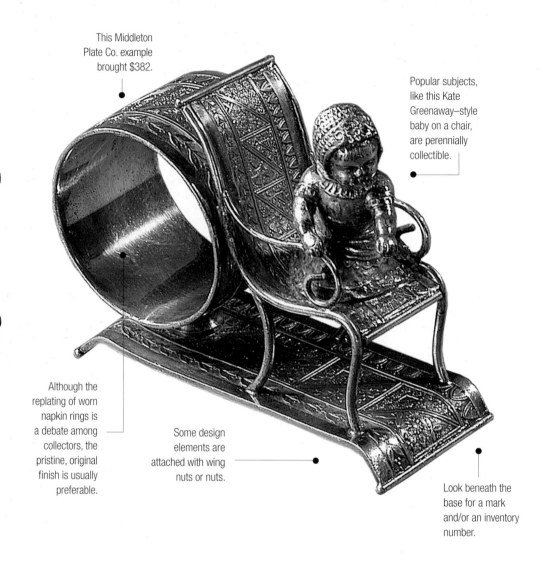

This Middleton Plate Co. example brought $382.

Popular subjects, like this Kate Greenaway–style baby on a chair, are perennially collectible.

Although the replating of worn napkin rings is a debate among collectors, the pristine, original finish is usually preferable.

Some design elements are attached with wing nuts or nuts.

Look beneath the base for a mark and/or an inventory number.

A Little Backstory

Napkin rings held linen dinner napkins, which were expected to be neatly refolded after each meal and replaced in a favorite ring. Figural napkin holders were beloved of late Victorians and have many fans today. As small and silvery sculptures (and by the way, American examples are always of silver plate, not sterling), they come in animal, vegetable, and mineral shapes as well as every type of cupid. They're still fun at dinner—even with paper napkins.

Good This example from the 1880s recalls the moment when all things Japanese were of interest to the West. But collectors of figural napkin rings seem not to be interested in the Aesthetic movement. Buyers let it go for a mere $40.

Better More desirable is this napkin ring mounted on a goat cart with movable wheels. It sold for $475. This example is stamped beneath the ring with one of the logos of the Britannia Meriden Company and came from a known collection.

Best For cupid collectors—and there are many—a prize. Less than 3 inches high with minor wear to its finish, this napkin ring has hearts and ribbons on the top and cupid reaching for an arrow. With a Reed & Barton mark, it sold for $690.

Look For

- Sterling silver figural holders, which are almost invariably British
- Figures and enhancements with particularly crisp detail
- Marks that identify the manufacturer. These are on the bottom, and are often in the form of a "coin" or button.
- An original, unreplated finish with very little wear
- Holiday themes

Stay Away From

- Cupids whose wings have broken off. (Cupids have wings. Cherubs never do.)
- Forgeries. Inventory numbers are available in specialized books or from still-extant companies.
- Prominent seams where the two ends of the napkin holder meet. Originals are suspicious.

Q & A

I know they can be expensive. Is there some way to tell if my own favorite subject is in my price range?

Figural napkin rings are so numerous and so highly collected that maybe the easiest way is just to buy one of the many picture-filled price books. Alternatively, pick the category that appeals to you—monkeys, maybe, or cherubs or Kate Greenaway figures—and start with the least expensive of them.

But how will I know which ones are rare and which are least expensive?

Rarity is pretty much the same for all collectibles, be they dolls, toys, golf clubs, or napkin rings. Those that were costliest when new were sold least frequently, and that means there are fewer of them today. Also, those that were poor sellers back then, perhaps because they were unusual or depicted difficult subjects, are also rare because they didn't sell well, either. Both histories guarantee rarity today. So if you come across an example that seems tremendously adorable or awfully unattractive, it will probably be rare. The most common examples are the least expensive.

I've seen some figural napkin rings that are dual- or even triple-purpose. Are they more valuable than the simpler ones?

Some napkin rings were combined with salt and pepper shakers, or with salt cellars and butter plates, and some actually incorporated glass or silver-plated bud vases. Unlike automobiles or cell phones, however, fancy "options" make them no more costly than the bare-bones napkin ring!

Look for makers' marks on the back of the head, under the hair, and on the doll's back.

Check for soiled areas and chipped paint.

The famous pin.

Clothes should be original, or from the 1930s.

Shirleys come in several sizes. This one is 13 inches.

Sold for $441.

A Little Backstory

Here's something to contemplate: the market for Shirley Temple dolls (or Mickey Mouse or Barbie, for that matter) will more or less disappear as their fan base moves on to that Great Dollhouse in the Sky. For the moment, however, there are plenty of collectors for the $6 million worth of dimpled Shirleys (her bottom is dimpled too) that have been sold since the 1930s. And they're pretty selective.

Q & A

What are the most popular celebrity dolls?
There are Jackie Robinson dolls and Jackie Kennedy dolls and Judy Garland dolls and Farrah Fawcett dolls, but Shirley seems to have been the most beloved of what we might term the huggable dolls. Barbie just isn't huggable.

Is that a pin on her outfit?
It's a circular celluloid pin with a picture of Shirley on it. Around the image of her curly head it reads "An original Shirley Temple doll." That authentication pin is so important to collectors that it's actually been faked.

If there were such a thing as the "perfect" vintage Shirley doll, what would she look like?
She'd be in her original box. Her sausage curls would be perfect, as would the little ribbon in her hair. Her outfit would be a rare one (like the cowgirl). And basically, she would never have been played with!

Look For

- Unusual outfits
- Original underwear (and *all* of it)
- Original shoes and socks, in pristine condition
- Hair that retains its original set (those sausage curls)
- Clear, uncrazed eyes
- A tag, proclaiming her "The World's Darling"
- Shirley accessories
- That celluloid pin

Stay Away From

- Shirleys (and Barbies) that have been loved too much
- Reproduction Shirleys, made in Germany, Japan, France, and the United States
- Soiled dolls
- American composition dolls
- Faded skin color
- Dolls with crazed eyes

Good A 17-inch vinyl doll, made by Ideal in 1957, is an example of the longevity of Shirley's popularity. She was a twenty-five-year-old woman when this doll was manufactured. The hair is a little mussed in back, and it has overall age discoloration, but mainly, because it's a late model, it brought a mere $77.

Better This 11-inch Shirley has tin eyes and is made of composition (a papier-mâché-like mixture of sawdust and glue, heated and poured into a mold). Over time, composition dolls tended to develop an overall network of fine cracks (crazing), an undesirable feature. She has her original mohair wig, but the seller is unsure if her dress is also original. Her underwear, shoes, and socks have been replaced. With all these drawbacks, she nevertheless sold for $330.

Best Also made of composition, and also wearing her original wig (though it's lost its set), this Shirley has lost her hat too. On top of it all, this 11-inch cowgirl Shirley has the cloudy eyes that seem to bedevil many vintage Shirleys. Still, she has her pin and her outfit is in good condition. She sold for $1,300.

American Shelf Clocks

The steeple shape is perhaps reminiscent of Gothic taste, or a church.

This 21½-inch-nineteenth-century shelf clock by Seth Thomas was sold in the thousands.

Look for chips on the face around the keyholes.

Note the herringbone ornament on this solid oak clock. The Victorians took such decoration for granted.

If there is gilding or painting, is it intact?

A Little Backstory

American shelf clocks are marvels of mass production. From Eli Terry (who sold $1 clocks) to Seth Thomas (who was even cheaper!), the versatile shelf clock kept decent time for either thirty hours or eight days, depending on which movement you bought. Shelf clock makers generally labeled their work, and the names of America's entrepreneurs can be found either on the clock face or on the back door.

Q & A

Didn't the Willard family make shelf clocks too?
Actually, around 1800, those well-known horological wizards, brothers Simon and Aaron Willard, produced the tall, handsome shelf clocks that are much prized by collectors today.

How do shelf clocks work?
Basically, they are spring driven and have a pendulum—like longcase clocks—but shorter, of course. All were meant to sit on a support, and throughout America, they were a staple of the well-furnished mantelpiece.

Is this a popular field?
So many of these clocks are available, and so many thousands were produced, that while many collectors like shelf clocks, the buyer today will still get a lot for his money: often, a solid rosewood or mahogany case, a decorated glass section, and of course, a timekeeper.

Is it important for an old clock to be working?
Serious clock collectors care more about the mechanics of a clock—its movement and "complications" (all the other things it can do in addition to indicating the hour)—than they do about appearances, so the answer depends upon how sophisticated a clock collector you hope to be. If you just want a cozy ornament, then you won't mind if it doesn't work. But if you don't like the idea of looking up from your paper every now and then to check the time, and finding your clock not ticking away, buy a good working movement.

Look For
- Unusual, attractive, cases
- The somewhat dainty mid-nineteenth-century clocks of Eli Terry
- Excellent condition (always key when quantities of the same item are available)
- Original keys
- A nicely painted glass door

Stay Away From
- Commonplace examples
- Missing veneers
- Reproductions
- Old clocks that have been given electric- or battery-driven movements

Good A pretty little 16-inch clock made by Atkins of Bristol, Connecticut, around 1860, this rosewood example—the wood of preference for the most costly of Victorian furniture—sold for $60.

Better This 22½-inch shelf clock, an unlabeled example made about twenty years later than the clock above, has a walnut case cut with a jigsaw and brought $100. With its gilt glass decoration and crenelated pediment, it epitomizes American mechanization run amok, and certainly unintentionally, explains the rise of the reactionary Arts and Crafts movement.

Best With its elegant lines and iconic American eagle finial, this circa 1815 Boston 35¼-inch-high. shelf clock looks—except for its reverse-painted upper panel and mirrored lower section—a bit like a New England chest-on-chest. In the painted glass panel (which is cracked), it's marked Aaron Willard/Boston. It brought $4,830.

Chinese Chippendale

Chinese Chippendale furniture was often lacquered in black, green, red, and (rarely) blue.

That octagonal design on the back appears in Chippendale's original furniture designs. You can easily research his engravings in reprints of his furniture directory.

Light colors usually indicate modern manufacture or—oh no—a repaint).

The fretwork on chair backs is easily broken. Check for missing and repaired bits, which (with so much going on) may not be immediately apparent.

These English chairs are eighteenth century (turn them over and look for signs of wear, darkening of exposed wood, and evidence of handwork).

They also have generous proportions and drop-in seats, suggesting that they may have been a special commission.

A Little Backstory

Chinese Chippendale, that gorgeous by-product of a 1741 travel book, was "invented" by English furniture designer Thomas Chippendale (the first nonmonarch to have a style named for him.) The craze it created in mid-eighteenth-century England prompted an aggrieved critic to write: "Every hovel for the cows has bells hanging at the corners." And while Chinese Chippendale is really a frothy side trip in the forward march of design, its pagodas and fretwork still lend their dollops of exoticism to our homes. We like it on anything. If only we still kept cows.

Good Mahogany Chinese Chippendale–style armchairs (watch out for that word "style") with the pattern squeezed into the openings below the arms and weak proportions brought $2,350.

Better Although this pair of Chippendale armchairs has super proportions, bells and whistles and *looks* really old, they are reproductions of eighteenth-century originals. They're spiffy enough, however (note those lively curved arms), to have brought $5,400.

Best Made circa 1765, and carved delicately with fine moldings and perfect proportions, these Chinese Chippendale chairs were possibly made in Thomas Chippendale's own workshop. At least two bidders seem to have agreed, since they sold for $217,000.

Look For

- Eighteenth-century furniture, mostly English, mostly elaborate, terrifically hard to find, and usually *expensive!*
- Early nineteenth-century Brighton Pavilion pieces incorporating brilliantly lacquered faux bamboo elements, lotuslike designs, or palm tree motifs. (Also costly.)
- Japanned clocks and secretaries Japanning—actually painting—was the European alternative to lacquering. Western cabinetmakers couldn't lacquer because they needed—and didn't have—lac beetles.

Stay Away From

- Damaged lacquer—a really difficult repair—and badly chipped paint too
- Clumsily executed carvings
- Missing elements of carving or fretwork
- Repainted anything

Q & A

Was Chinese Chippendale furniture actually made in China? And what's the difference between it and regular Chippendale?
Thomas Chippendale was already famous for elegant mahogany Chippendale furniture when he applied the newly popular chinoiserie to his quintessentially English wares. And while—for economy's sake—he might have preferred to have his furniture made in the Far East, in 1750s London, only lacquer and porcelain "smalls" were being shipped to the West.

What's the difference between Chinese furniture and Chinese Chippendale furniture?
Early Chinese furniture is austere. It's teak or ebony and strongly linear with not much carving. Chippendale's "Chinese" designs, on the other hand, are rococo and embellished with all sorts of architectural details borrowed from China. Some are more successful than others. All are busy.

Some of the pieces I've seen, though, look fairly restrained.
The more restrained designs are later takes on the whimsical furnishings of the Brighton Pavilion, an exotic, early nineteenth-century palace built for the Prince Regent. Mid-eighteenth-century furnishings were *so* fancy, however, that in 1756, one observer wrote, "Every chair in an apartment . . . must be Chinese: the walls covered with Chinese paper filled with figures which resemble nothing in God's creation, and which a prudent nation would prohibit for the sake of pregnant women."

Is Chinese Chippendale more expensive than "plain" furniture?
Usually it is, because every step that's added to the furniture-making process makes the finished product more expensive. A pagoda pediment on a mirror, tiny bells dangling on corners, carved herons, and lots of latticework will make any piece—old or new—pricier.

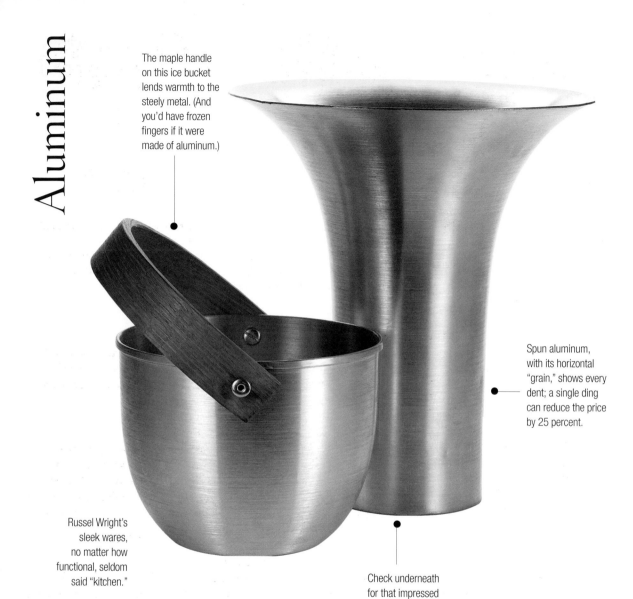

Aluminum

The maple handle on this ice bucket lends warmth to the steely metal. (And you'd have frozen fingers if it were made of aluminum.)

Spun aluminum, with its horizontal "grain," shows every dent; a single ding can reduce the price by 25 percent.

Russel Wright's sleek wares, no matter how functional, seldom said "kitchen."

Check underneath for that impressed maker's mark.

A Little Backstory

Here's what you can do with lightweight, cool aluminum: hammer it, print on it, color it with jewel tones, put ice in it, put ice in it and write your initials on the condensation. It makes nice cookware too, although once it left the kitchen, it became far more interesting. Aluminum giftware was in its glory until World War II; then it all went to war. Subtle and sophisticated, it's seriously taken for granted. And shouldn't be.

Good These gorgeously colored anodized Colorama sherbet cups with glass liners are mint, and come in their original box. New in the 1950s, they retailed for $8.50; today, they're $85.

Better Kensington spun wares were Alcoa's answer to Russel Wright. This 15-inch 1930s charger with its circlet of embossed inlaid brass and incised compass rose is, sadly, scratched and marred, so it's only $95.

Best At $125, this graceful hammered Buenilum compote is a bargain when compared with the 1940s sterling silver it hoped to replace. (There's even a matching pair of candlesticks.)

Look For

- Streamlined designs by Richard Neutra and Russel Wright (whose name will be impressed on the bottom)
- The wares of Lurell E. Guild, who designed sophisticated alternatives to silver for Kensington
- Large pieces, like wastebaskets and magazine racks
- Heavyweight aluminum, often of early manufacture and usually of superior quality
- Privately commissioned pieces like lamps or tables

Stay Away From

- Pitted aluminum or any aluminum with a white haze (usually the effect of salt exposure)
- Scratches or tiny dents on spun-finished aluminum—though dents can be repaired
- Scratched anodized aluminum, which is irreparable
- Tumblers damaged by exposure to acidic liquids
- All those much-too-lightweight 1950s decorative wares that were sold in five-and-tens

Q & A

How can you tell aluminum from other metals—brushed stainless steel, for instance?
Stainless steel is a good deal heavier than aluminum. It isn't hammered like aluminum, and it's not as likely to show nasty scratches, whereas aluminum is incredibly soft.

Who are the popular manufacturers or designers?
In hammered aluminum, collectors look for Arthur Armour's pieces and those of the Wendell August Forge, which specialized in handmade items. The designs of Frederic Buehner (which he modestly called Buenilum) are traditional and resemble Georg Jensen silver. For spun aluminum, wares by Kensington, an Alcoa subsidiary, and work by Russel Wright are standouts.

Why is some aluminum hammered?
There are experts who attribute it to the fact that the first commercial designers in the 1930s were accustomed to working in wrought iron, which is usually hammered. Some think it was an aesthetic choice, that the hammering makes it handsomer. I sometimes suspect it was an excellent way to hide potential scratches.

Gift and tablewares in aluminum seem so reasonable today. Were they ever expensive?
Even when the metal was "new" in the 1850s, and such a novelty that it was occasionally combined with gold, it still sold for less than silver. Ladies' fans were fashioned in aluminum, and René Lalique made jewelry with it, but the metal was never truly costly.

Dog Paintings

Size counts. This is a big painting, 26 x 48 inches.

The signature should resemble others by the artist, in this instance, Edmund Osthaus.

A date is considered a plus.

The specific pointers are identified in the materials with this painting and were noted examples of their breed.

A Little Backstory

Dog painters tend to specialize in canines. As is the case with all types of artists, some are better than others (as are their subjects). But those subjects—terriers, hounds, working dogs, and so on—are currently so popular that they occasion their own private auctions: dogs only. With the exception of those hard-to-live-with pictures of hunting dogs attacking prey, there are very few dog paintings that don't find a home.

Q & A

Do the same rules apply for these pictures as for paintings in general?
Absolutely. You have to consider condition, provenance, age, artist, and rarity, but in this case, you might also want to consider their "cute" and "fashion" quotients. Puppy pictures have "cute" nailed down. But it's also nice if those puppies are currently in fashion. In the 1970s, for instance, very few people knew what a Jack Russell terrier was. Today, they're shown at major American dog shows (as Parson Russell terriers), and there are many new collectors for the paintings of those little terrors . . . terriers.

Even if they're painted by mediocre artists?
Even then. And especially if the image has some age.

And how do I know if I'm looking at the work of a mediocre artist?
At one time, novice collectors were told to look at hands. If the hands were well depicted, the painting was likely to be a good one. With dog paintings, artistry counts highly too (although paws won't tell you much). Does the fur look real? Is the facial expression accurate and appealing? Is the background part of the image, or just a stage prop? Is the picture too sweetly sentimental?

Look For
- Your favorite dogs (of course)
- Other people's favorite dogs
- An original frame
- The signature of a well-known animal painter, such as Arthur Wardle, Sir Alfred Munnings, and Edwin Henry Landseer (English) or Edmund Osthaus, Arthur Fitzwilliam Tait, and Percival Rosseau (American)
- The typical subject for a particular artist. For example, if an artist is particularly noted for his depictions of sporting dogs, his painting of a Pomeranian is likely to be less sought after.
- Good folk paintings, often unsigned

Stay Away From
- The work of amateurs, of which there is a great deal, little girls of all eras being particularly fond of painting their favorite pets. (Unless they're too charming to pass up!)
- Copies of well-known paintings
- Forged signatures
- Dubious attributions, often accompanied by an impressive engraved brass plate attached to the frame
- Any painting with the canvas stapled to the frame

Good This appealing portrait of a little terrier, approximately 22 x 27 inches, is oil on canvas, and signed "L. Mellinger '95." While it looks like it was copied from a photograph, it's nicely executed (although it could have done with a better background). Because today's buyers want their nineteenth-century paintings to be signed by known artists, this little picture brought only $708.

Better This sentimental painting is unsigned, but at 15½ x 12 inches it's slightly larger than the image above, and besides being well painted, the chipper Maltese has decorative pompoms and a sweet expression. His "pedigree" (he comes from the collection of a marquis) helped him fetch $5,900.

Best This obviously well fed and spoiled little terrier (on a silken wing chair) is an unusual subject for Alfred Munnings, an artist best known for his horse pictures. At 16 x 14 inches, the painting is a good size, maybe a little small, and might almost be a relative of that little guy who's "good." Not quite, though, because its atypical subject (for Munnings) didn't keep it from selling for $42,000.

The dress indicates an eighteenth-century origin, but in fact, it's a late-nineteenth-century copy of a famed eighteenth-century piece.

The painting and detail are exceptionally well done. Avoid perfunctory work.

Check fingers and hands (or tips of horns). Often, they are damaged.

This is a large figure, 17 inches tall. In nineteenth-century wares, larger is generally better.

Check the back and the bottom for marks (and be very dubious). This example *is* marked with Meissen's blue crossed swords, but the original is well known, and the glazes and colors here are harsh in comparison.

A Little Backstory

Nineteenth-century Continental porcelain figures owe everything to eighteenth-century Meissen, the first European porcelain factory to discover the formula for hard-paste porcelain. Meissen figures were of superb quality and the company was therefore the most fashionable of the German manufacturers. All of Europe copied its wares.

Q & A

How do I tell eighteenth-century from nineteenth-century figures?
Don't look to find eighteenth-century pieces at a local flea market, but if you're shopping at antiques stores, or online, know that the newer figures will usually be more flamboyant, with more and richer gilding, and will be trying harder to be a status symbol.

Is Dresden the same as Meissen?
Actually not, although many people confuse the two. Dresden isn't far from Meissen, and in the nineteenth century, at least forty factories, large and small, made hard-paste copies of its neighbor's famous wares.

What about fakes?
There are plenty of fakes to worry about, especially of Meissen and Sèvres, the great French porcelain factory. Samson in Paris did excellent copies of *all* the best porcelains, and even added chemicals to make its hard-paste look like soft paste. Interestingly, there are collectors of Samson itself.

What about prices for nineteenth-century figures?
Pretty as they are, there's not much interest in them these days. Most are simply casting an eye back at the past rather than moving the medium forward, and that lack of originality prevents their being considered Art, with a capital A.

Look For
- Large figures
- Tableaux of several figures
- The works of Samson (see above)
- Unusual subjects, such as exotic animals
- Meissen's own nineteenth-century figures (which may be copies of its eighteenth-century wares) are incised on the base with cursive numbers of a larger size than the accompanying serif numbers.
- Glazed concave bases, which are typical of nineteenth-century wares

Stay Away From
- The all-too-common figures with generically "pretty" features
- Repairs
- Clumsily modeled figures
- Pale and insipid coloring

Good The sort of Renaissance costume on this very large, 17-inch bisque (unglazed) porcelain figure is typical of its late-nineteenth-century date, the era of Renaissance Revival. It is unmarked, and has a hairline crack running from the base to the knee, both of which account for its $150 selling price.

Better This 8¾-inch Continental lap dog (a Bolognese) on a red cushion is an unmarked copy of a famous Meissen figure. It's well done enough to have been produced by Samson, but currently, adorable nineteenth-century dogs don't really need much pedigree to sell for $1,000.

Best This Meissen ewer, thoroughly encrusted with mermaids, seahorses, Neptune, fish, dolphins, and turtles, exemplifies both the best and worst of nineteenth-century European porcelain. It may be a 26-inch tour de force of modeling and workmanship, but for this eminent old factory, it's also a misguided attempt at "modernity." (It was late-nineteenth-century modern.) Despite chips and restorations, the size and maker of this piece helped it sell for $5,500.

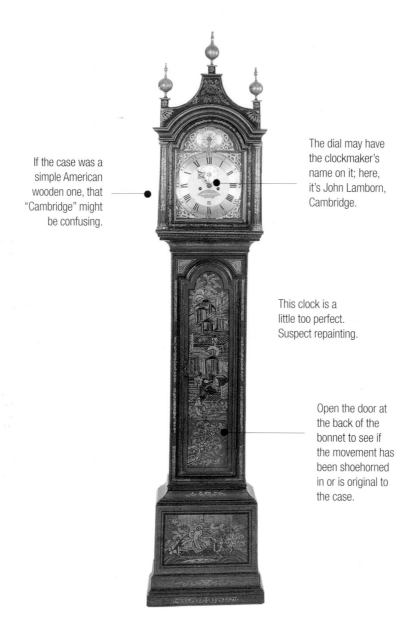

If the case was a simple American wooden one, that "Cambridge" might be confusing.

The dial may have the clockmaker's name on it; here, it's John Lamborn, Cambridge.

This clock is a little too perfect. Suspect repainting.

Open the door at the back of the bonnet to see if the movement has been shoehorned in or is original to the case.

A Little Backstory

Tall case clocks are furniture as much as they are timepieces. And while true clock collectors are predominantly interested in the movement of a clock, decorators may be more interested in appearances. For that reason, we are considering here tall case clocks in which the externals are sometimes more elaborate than the internals.

Q & A

Does this mean that we should judge the clock case the way we'd judge a piece of furniture?
Absolutely. Are the proportions right? Does the size of the bonnet overwhelm the other two elements? Have there been many replaced parts or repairs to original wood elements? If the case is japanned, has there been much repainting?

What does "japanned" mean?
Japanned decoration was popular in England from the end of the seventeenth century into the early eighteenth century. It was developed as a substitute for hard-to-get Chinese lacquer, but unlike the original, it contained no lac from beetles. It is essentially paint, and was done in black, red, cream, green, and, occasionally, blue.

What other types of decoration were common?
Depending on the country and era of its manufacture, a wooden clock case might have elaborate floral inlay; be made of a single wood, such as mahogany; be embellished with carving; or be sedately inlaid with fine lines composed of other, usually lighter, woods, called "stringing."

Look For

- Japanned patterns that were popular in a given era that will help you home in on age. For example, a particular vase of flowers on the door might be known to have been copied from a well-known treatise on japanning.
- The shape of the bonnet is a big help in identifying age.
- A maker's name on the face of the clock, or on a brass plate on its back
- Movements by important makers
- The happy accident of the really good movement in a highly decorative case

Stay Away From

- Later inlay that attempts to dress up an otherwise plain case
- Replaced elements or missing feet
- Extensive repainting of the japanning
- A movement and case that weren't "born together," often recognizable by some visible rejiggering of the wooden support that holds the movement on the inside of the bonnet
- Ghosts indicating old supports
- Badly chipped or missing japanning
- Too-tall clocks (unless they fit in your room)

Good This marquetry inlaid clock looks very much like the Dutch clocks of the early eighteenth century, but it's actually a nineteenth-century example, though it *is* Dutch. The hood is lacking its corner finials, there are cracks in the case (America's central heating, no doubt) and the dinky little finial on very top can't be original! It sold for $3,200.

Better Floral bouquets are inlaid on a late-seventeenth-century English clock that is, naturally, more restrained than the Dutch example above. There seems to be no maker's label on the face, and no mention is made of a maker in the auction catalogue. Despite being in good condition, of a practical size (it's 86 inches high), and having good looks, it brought a mere $8,400.

Best Japanned tall case clocks, while not necessarily more desirable than inlaid clocks, can sometimes be pricey. This example is "best" because in addition to its case being in perfect condition, its movement is by a known seventeenth-century clockmaker. And this clock chimes not just on the hour or half hour, but on the quarter hour as well. Perhaps equally important, it comes from the home of a well-known American socialite, and it sold for $57,360.

Suzanis

The face of this vintage suzani looks unworn, but if dyes are faded, check the back for patches.

The variations in the curly black wreaths that set off the sunburst medallions indicate handwork.

Right down the middle, where two strips join, there's visible fudging of the seam.

The dyes have faded unevenly. This eggplant and orange combination seems astonishingly sophisticated!

A Little Backstory

What *is* a suzani, anyway? A tropical storm? A sleek foreign car? (If it's in this book, you know it's neither.) It's actually the Central Asian equivalent of grandma's heirloom quilt: handmade, hand stitched, and handed down. It's cloth, lavishly embroidered (suzani means "needle" in Persian), which, like our own quilts, was used to cover beds and cribs as well as tables, horses, and walls. Talented needlewomen produced this brilliant Folk Art for centuries, but only for themselves. When the Iron Curtain lifted, there they were: thousands of artful, useful (emphasis on the first syllable) suzanis.

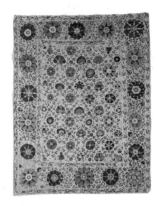

Good At approximately 8½ x 6 feet, this nineteenth-century silk suzani has several problems, beginning with a murky background that dampens its hues. But it's also torn and has a hole right in the middle, so it sold for $350.

Better This 52 x 52-inch example of a mid-nineteenth-century suzani from Central Asia has embroidery losses in the border and a few stains, but its bold design and cheerful coloration are what buyers want and it brought $2,489.

Best A sophisticated pattern and beautifully conceived and executed detail drove the selling price of this 7-foot 10-inch x 5 foot 11-inch Central Asian suzani (with pinholes and stains) to $18,750. It didn't hurt that it came from a Getty collection.

Look For

- Antique suzanis, which often sell in the $2,000 to $4,000 range
- Outstanding needlework (although the work on most suzanis is breathtaking). Some examples have been overstiched, so that like velvet, they reveal different shadings in different lights.
- Improvisations within a repeated pattern. In other words, designs that vary from one another in exciting ways, rather like a jazz musician's riff on a single musical passage.
- Large medallion suzanis from the early to mid-nineteenth century

Stay Away From

- Worn suzanis (unless you find yourself in love with one). Hold them up to the light to check for holes and wear.
- Faded examples (don't overexpose your own to sunlight!)
- Machine-made suzanis, which are quite regular and perfect, and probably produced in large numbers
- Overly bright colors, which are often synthetic
- Suzani fragments, unless you want to frame them, or (as one acquaintance does) hot-glue them to sofas and chairs

Q & A

How do they do that amazing embroidery?
The background fabric, usually a cotton-silk blend, is taken first to a local "designer," who bastes four or six narrow widths together and draws her design on the whole. Then it's taken apart again, and each female member of the family embroiders a separate strip. When all are complete, the piece is reassembled. But the designs don't always line up, which gives the suzani its endearing flaws.

The work is so intricate. Is it an ancient skill?
Because suzanis were used until they were threadbare, the oldest ones we know of are from the eighteenth century. Their designs, however those meandering grapevines and tulips—can be traced back to ancient Greece and the Ottoman Empire, and the dyes, of course, were natural, the colors being created from pomegranate juice, walnuts, and indigo.

They remind me a lot of oriental rugs.
In fact, they are very much embroidered versions of hand-loomed rugs. Many of the motifs—the palmette, the tulip, the teardrop-shaped *botah* that we associate with paisleys—are familiar from carpets, but instead of being made on looms, the stylized, finely stitched designs of suzanis are worked with a kind of small crochet hook.

How would I tell the old ones from the new ones?
Some of the newer suzanis are worked on colored backgrounds—red, pink, yellow, and occasionally violet—while the older ones are on neutral grounds. In addition, many from the late nineteenth and early twentieth century were colored with synthetic dyes that seem dull now when compared with those made with natural dyes.

Art Glass Compotes

Hold small pieces like this up to the light to look for mends or cracks. This piece sold for $1,200.

This piece is completely unmarked, although it would be instantly recognizable to art glass collectors as twentieth-century Murano glass, the work of Salvatore Salviati.

At 9¼ inches, it's a standard compote size.

Look beneath the foot or around the outside of the piece for an incised signature or even, on occasion, a paper label.

A Little Backstory

Toward the end of the nineteenth century, new glassmaking techniques were popularized by artists such as American Louis Comfort Tiffany and Frenchman René Lalique. They, and others like them, created art glass.

Art glass can be mold blown (visualize a liquid bubble of glass being blown by mouth into a mold) or free blown (no mold, just lungs, pincers, and talent). The virtuoso skills of these innovators, seen in thousands of pieces of amazing glass, have been favorites with collectors since the 1960s.

Q & A

How do I tell art glass from other glass?
Shapes are generally swirling and naturalistic, and the glass may be colored with iridescent or opalescent shadings (although Lalique preferred frosted and clear). As the twentieth century progressed, the colors of art glass became crisper, and Art Deco designs—female forms, gazelles, jazz images—were engraved on clear or single-color wares.

Is carnival glass art glass? It's iridescent and colorful.
No. Carnival glass, made in the 1930s, was a mass-produced alternative made for those who liked the appearance of art glass, but (and most particularly during the Depression era) couldn't afford it.

Isn't art glass usually signed by the maker?
It is, and that's a real danger for the novice who depends too much on signatures and too little on scholarship. Collecting is not always easy. Fakes and reproductions lie in wait to trip us up.

Look For

- Aurene and Cluthra glass from Steuben, and early Steuben pieces signed Carder
- Tiffany glass, which is usually signed but often faked
- European glass from Galle, Daum, and Lalique
- Large pieces, which are always more valuable, simply for having survived, if nothing else
- Uncommon shapes from the well-known manufacturers, or better yet, shapes that are one of a kind

Stay Away From

- Bubbles in glass, which can be part of the design or not. Pass on glass that has unintentional bubbles in the "metal" (the technical term for glass)
- Overlarge Steuben marks or fleur-de-lis. These are often forgeries.
- Crudely executed engraving
- All the usual caveats about chips or mended chips, and breaks or mended breaks
- Repaired glass. It has lost most, if not all, of its value.

Good Many glass companies jumped on the Tiffany bandwagon. Quezal, of New York City, was a follower, not a leader, and collectors know the difference. This iridescent, 5-inch-high gold compote is signed Quezal beneath the foot and sold for $300.

Better Here's the real McCoy, a small (4¼ inches) compote decorated with a green "pulled feather" motif on opalescent glass. Signed and numbered on the underside of the foot, it's pretty, though common, and it's not a thrilling example of Tiffany's glass. Advanced collectors want to be thrilled. It brought $1,668.

Best Signed not on the foot but on the bottom of the bowl, this equally small (just under 5 inches), colorless, and well-designed Lalique compote sold for $5,500. It has finely carved glass handles.

Were the top and bottom born together? Look for ghosts of missing elements underneath and screw holes.

Is the top veneered or is it solid wood?

Brass inlaid calamander wood is very sophisticated.

Carving should be well defined and crisp.

Beneath the table top you might also find the smudged fingerprints of the gentlemen who periodically wheeled it into playing position.

The underside should be lighter in color than those parts exposed to air, centuries of dusting, dirt, and sweaty hands.

Damaged or missing veneers on edges can be easily repaired, as can missing felt.

English Regency Card Tables

A Little Backstory

The English Regency card table was designed to enhance, with late Georgian chic, one's card game. The card table form was developed in the late seventeenth century, metamorphosing through the eighteenth and nineteenth centuries into the card table of today, the one that folds up. The tables that follow stood between two windows or against a wall, to be pulled out when needed, and opened to reveal a felt covered playing surface that often swiveled. It seated four. Beneath the top, there might also be a compartment for storing cards and game pieces.

Q & A

What exactly is it that makes these tables Regency?
This is their *era*. It's named for the period from 1811 to 1820, when the ruler of Britain was the "mad" George III's son, the Prince Regent; it actually began in the late eighteenth century and ended in the 1840s. Their *style* is neoclassical. Paw feet, animal head masks, and Grecian motifs like lyres and laurel wreaths were common neoclassical motifs.

Those seem like odd motifs. Why were they popular?
The discovery of Pompeii and Herculaneum in the eighteenth century affected not just architecture and fashion, but everyday furnishings such as tables and teacups.

Why do so many of these tables roll on wheels?
Those wheels are called casters, and they were installed to allow the tables to be easily moved to a location near the light. Before electricity, furniture was commonly moved around rooms, either to follow the daylight or to be closer to the fireplace.

Look For

- The table top shape, which might be a plain rectangle, a semicircle, serpentine, or rectangle with rounded corners. Collectors prefer an elegantly shaped top, which is more difficult and costly to make.
- Carved decoration
- Brass inlay
- Unusually beautiful casters
- Matched veneers
- Expensive or rare woods, such as calamander (a zebra-striped species of ebony) or rosewood (the name refers to its scent when cut)

Stay Away From

- Mismatched tops and bottoms
- Split or warped wood tops
- The heavy later styles
- Pedestal tables, which are less popular than tables with four legs

Good This William IV card table (second quarter of the nineteenth century) is nicely proportioned, has some carving, and is veneered in rosewood. The missing veneer on the edge would be unimportant were this an earlier, more elaborate, more decorative example. It sold for a mere $480.

Better This very plain early nineteenth-century table is inlaid with stained fruitwood. Its rounded corners and gracefully splayed legs (plus its actually *having* legs) make it, at $1,445, more highly sought after than the preceding example.

Best This table is "best" because it sort of cheated. It was once the property of Queen Elizabeth's sister, Princess Margaret, and its celebrity adds unwarranted value. Not that this isn't a pretty example, but its barrel column and possibly its support have been replaced, and the top is split. The brass inlay, trim, and carving are nice, but without that royal provenance, this would simply be a "better" table.

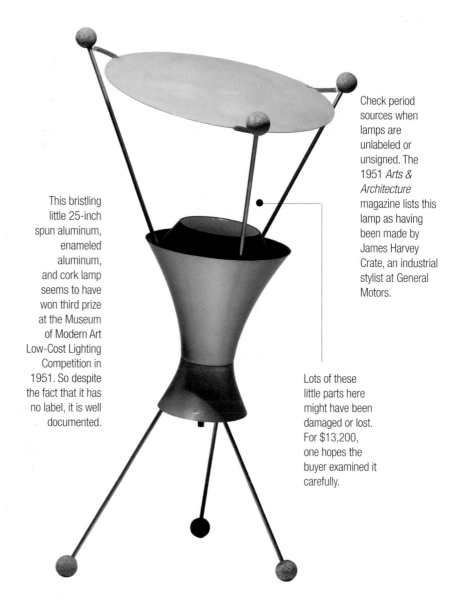

Check period sources when lamps are unlabeled or unsigned. The 1951 *Arts & Architecture* magazine lists this lamp as having been made by James Harvey Crate, an industrial stylist at General Motors.

This bristling little 25-inch spun aluminum, enameled aluminum, and cork lamp seems to have won third prize at the Museum of Modern Art Low-Cost Lighting Competition in 1951. So despite the fact that it has no label, it is well documented.

Lots of these little parts here might have been damaged or lost. For $13,200, one hopes the buyer examined it carefully.

A Little Backstory

Lighting, an eccentric little subdivision of furniture manufacture, follows innovation in design; it doesn't lead. The fertile imaginations of the 1950s and 1960s came up with some rather amazing lamps for ceiling and wall, table and floor. Some were so strange and even (outer) spacey that they were lampooned in the cartoons of the time. Others weren't funny, perhaps, but were even stranger.

Q & A

Why were the fifties a hotbed of kitsch?
With the victorious ending of the Second World War, Europeans and Americans were truly giddy with peace. Anything seemed possible in lives that were freed, at last, from ration books and flattened tin cans (collected for the war effort), and anything was run up the flagpole. If you couldn't completely refurnish that brand-new ranch house, at least you could buy a new lamp.

Where did all these influences come from?
Serious influences were the hanging mobiles of artist Alexander Calder and the paintings of Piet Mondrian. A lot less serious were omnipresent flying saucer sightings, *Sputnik* with its many antennae, and postwar advances in the plastics industry.

If I buy a midcentury lamp, should I expect it to work?
That's not always included in the price, although if it *does* work these many decades later, the wiring might be unsafe. It's easy enough to have a lamp rewired, of course, and it won't affect its resale value should you decide that after all, you'd rather have halogen.

Look For

- Examples of high-style 1930s lighting
- Italian floor lamps from the 1950s, especially those by Castiglioni
- Chandeliers and lamps by influential Danish architect Poul Henningsen, some of which may be recognized by the fact that they look very much like artichokes
- Lighting by American designer George Nelson, head designer for Herman Miller, Inc.
- Whimsy in combination with the most modern of materials: aluminum, plastic, and stainless steel
- Documented prize-winning designs

Stay Away From

- Plastic that has discolored or cracked from heat
- Chipped enamel
- Badly corroded or pitted metal
- Reproductions, which may *eventually* acquire some value, but which will never have the cachet of an original
- Missing parts, even seemingly insignificant bits such as finials
- Scary wiring

Good In the following highly select group of table lamps, this merely "good" example sold for $4,000 because it's the 1931 design in enameled steel, frosted glass, brass, bakelite, and enameled aluminum of Poul Henningsen. It measures 17½ inches high x 13¾ inches in diameter.

Better A pair of 11-inch-tall dressing table lamps by Jacques Adnet have the added advantage of being made with labeled crystal balls by the famous French glass manufacturer Baccarat. Note that the wire doesn't go through the glass, definitely an advantage with a lamp base that has value. The pair brought $15,600.

Best This 1969 plastic mushroom lamp by Verner Panton is a prototype, and the lacquered maple base you see here was not used in the final commerical design. Why did this sell for $14,400? It has a pleasingly simple shape and substantial size (23½ inches), but primarily because it's a prototype.

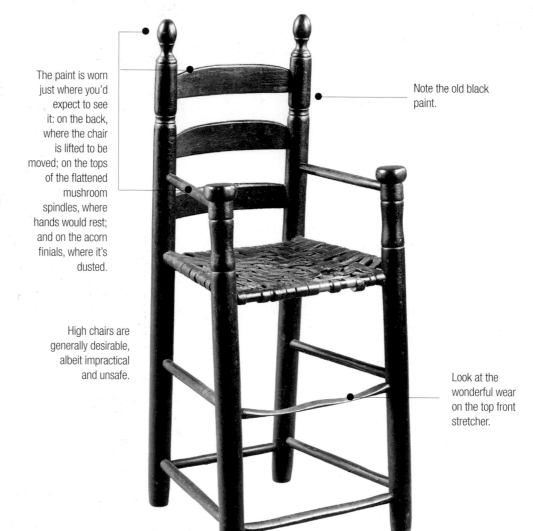

The paint is worn just where you'd expect to see it: on the back, where the chair is lifted to be moved; on the tops of the flattened mushroom spindles, where hands would rest; and on the acorn finials, where it's dusted.

Note the old black paint.

High chairs are generally desirable, albeit impractical and unsafe.

Look at the wonderful wear on the top front stretcher.

A Little Backstory

Full disclosure: You're not going to find much in the way of Pilgrim-century furniture in your local antique store. Or in a barn in Salem, Massachusetts, or even at a major Americana auction in New York. Survivals of this furniture are few, to begin with, and most of the really great pieces are safely in museums. But because so many rural chairs made in the nineteenth century can look very much like seventeenth-century chairs, it's a good idea to know what the genuinely old ones look like.

Q & A

How do Pilgrim-century chairs differ in design from later chairs?
Exactly the way we like to believe the Pilgrims themselves were—they're upright and foursquare. And like English Jacobean furniture, which they resemble, the components are turned, and the best of them are veritable symphonies of turned spindles. The chair seats are usually woven rush, or (ouch) wooden plank.

And how do they differ in appearance?
Seventeenth-century chairs are usually oak but there are maple examples because America's joiners, who weren't quite cabinetmakers yet, used whatever woods were handy. These old chairs will, of course, show signs of wear on the armrests, the bottoms of legs, and the top rails, but do be careful: They've been faked for at least a century, and now even the fakes show wear.

What's the difference between Brewster chairs and Carver chairs?
Both were named for elders of the Plymouth Colony, but Brewster chairs have elaborate spindles only on the back, while Carvers have additional spindles below the arms and seat. This type of chair is also called a great chair.

Where do these chairs come from?
They come, of course, from New England, which accounts for this type of furniture being called Pilgrim furniture. Technically, however, it should be called American Jacobean furniture.

Look For

- Uprights that are fairly thick with complex turnings
- Replaced seats. This may be one of the few instances where you *want* to see a replacement, because the original seats have almost never survived.
- The very well-made and branded Wallace Nutting copies from the 1920s, which have become collectibles in their own right.
- Nicely worn-down feet

Stay Away From

- Cut-down legs
- Too many missing spindles or rails
- Fakes
- A chair (or any antique, for that matter) that is more money than you're comfortable with, unless you consult an expert
- Uniform wear where you'd expect to find it, like the rail on which you rest your feet or the places where the hands rest on the arms. Few old chairs wear evenly.

Good Here's an awkward (and probably uncomfortable) corner chair with two of its three legs having been added to, and some of its rails possibly replaced. Nevertheless, it is late seventeenth century, and certainly worth the $800 it sold for.

Better What a gorgeous Carver chair. Except it's an "I wish I were a Brewster chair." Attributed to Wallace Nutting (but not labeled), the rear legs on this birch example from the twentieth century have been shortened and the finish is worn; nevertheless, it brought $3,750 because it's Nutting and, well, gorgeous.

Best Made of ash, and hardly the most decorative of Pilgrim-era chairs, this example is a testimony to the importance of provenance. It descended in a well-documented line from John Alden, the twenty-two-year-old hero of America's first romance. The feet are properly worn (those plastic buttons are OK), the tops of the armrests have been worn down by time, and all is smooth because it was endlessly dusted. The seat, of course, is replaced. Estimated to sell for $8,000 to $12,000, it brought $26,000.

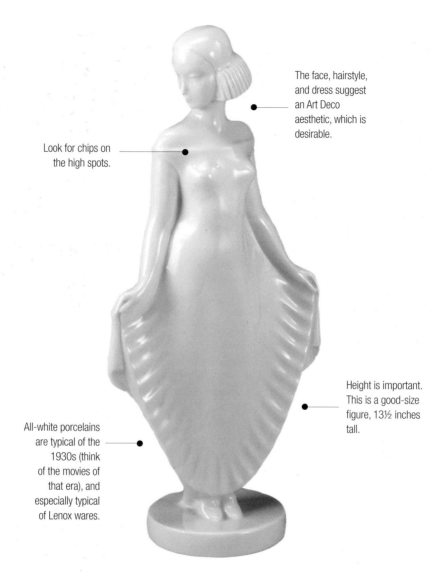

The face, hairstyle, and dress suggest an Art Deco aesthetic, which is desirable.

Look for chips on the high spots.

Height is important. This is a good-size figure, 13½ inches tall.

All-white porcelains are typical of the 1930s (think of the movies of that era), and especially typical of Lenox wares.

A Little Backstory

With the exception of two or three famous names, there's little creative to recommend in twentieth-century American porcelain. Of course, there has never been a Meissen or a Sèvres in the United States, so while Americans liked collecting porcelain, especially in the nineteenth century, they always preferred European wares. Only the Lenox factory stood out from the crowd among American manufacturers. (And Lenox descended from Ireland's Belleek.) America's studio potters, however, rank with the best in the world.

Q & A

How is American porcelain marked?
It won't all be marked "Made in USA," a labeling that didn't come into general use until the 1920s. Any mark, usually a logo of some sort, will be impressed into the porcelain, in relief or printed. You may have to check a book of porcelain marks, where you'll find, for instance, that Lenox can also be marked "CAC" (Ceramic Art Company). This was its earliest name. Collectors look for the early examples.

What are some of the other famous names you mentioned?
Taxile Doat was a famous ceramicist in early twentieth-century France. He was working for Sèvres when he was invited to the United States to be the director of the University City Pottery in Saint Louis, Missouri. Adelaide Robineau's work (she was based in Syracuse, New York) was inventive and imaginative. Her ceramics from the first quarter of the twentieth century look like no one else's: She carved her pieces, played with glazes, or pierced the clay—all to outstanding effect.

Why do you think there isn't more American porcelain?
With the arrival of the Art Deco style after the First World War, interest turned to the arts of Africa and to the Egyptian aesthetic. Thus it became more primitive, and primitive in ceramics equals pottery, not porcelain. Almost all the exciting work in ceramics in twentieth-century America was done in earthenware and stoneware.

Look For

- Figures with finely executed detail
- Signatures or monograms, in addition to factory logos
- The mark "UC/19../TD," which seems cryptic unless you know it stands for "University City/the year/Taxile Doat"
- Eggshell-thin pierced porcelains. *Very* rare, but typical of those done by Robineau, whose mark is "AR," in a circular monogram

Stay Away From

- Cracks and chips, unless the pieces are so rare they might never be found in perfect condition
- Repairs, because the newer a piece of porcelain is, the more likely it is to have been made in large batches, meaning that there are plenty of perfect examples still to be had
- Ill-defined details such as poorly delineated hair and hands
- Japanese copies of anything

Good These creamy Lenox porcelain demitasse cups in their filigree sterling holders must have been immensely popular as wedding gifts in the early to mid-twentieth century, because you'll see them everywhere. These two, from a group of twelve, in their fitted case, brought only $236 at auction, which may have been due to the fact that five saucers are missing from the set and at least one of the silver holders is a mismatch.

Better A small (5¾ inches wide) University City dish made in 1914, the era of Taxile Doat, is distinctly Japanesque. Decorated with vibrant marine life and blue "jewels," it has several long firing cracks. It is marked, however (UC/1914/TD), and sold for $940.

Best By Adelaide Robineau, this 7-inch-tall bud vase is covered in a crystalline amber glaze. Robineau preferred to make hand-thrown pieces, and this is a typical example (although it does seem to lean a little to the left). It is signed "AR," with a circular stamp, and brought $9,000.

Toast Racks

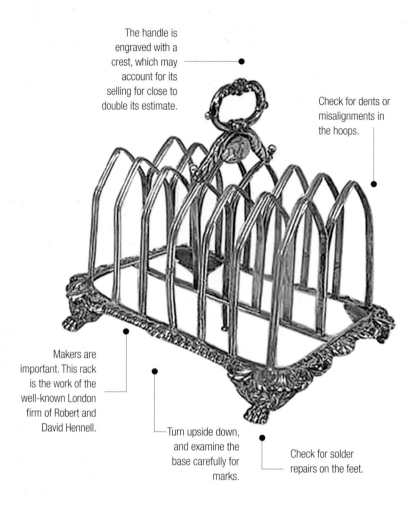

The handle is engraved with a crest, which may account for its selling for close to double its estimate.

Check for dents or misalignments in the hoops.

Makers are important. This rack is the work of the well-known London firm of Robert and David Hennell.

Turn upside down, and examine the base carefully for marks.

Check for solder repairs on the feet.

A Little Backstory

The English have obviously never minded eating cold toast. There can be no other explanation for the prevalence, in Great Britain, of the silver toast rack. Americans may not have taken to the toast, but they do like the rack part for holding mail. And they're good for (tiny collections of) CDs, as well. Certainly, there are plenty of collectors, here and there, vying for this pretty nonnecessity.

Good This piece looks as if it were designed by great English innovator Christopher Dresser, and it bears English hallmarks. The auctioneer gave it a "Dresser" estimate of $400–$600 and it brought a scary $275, too much for an ordinary toast rack and too little for the real McCoy.

Better This one, a more distinctly Aesthetic era style toast rack than the "good example," is stamped with the mark of Hukin & Heath, an English firm that employed Dresser from 1878 to 1881. This *is* a Dresser toast rack, but repaired and only worth $350.

Best This toast rack is only silver plate, but bears the facsimile signature of Christopher Dresser; *and* the design appears in James Dixon's (the manufacturer) catalogue. Twenty years ago this might not have been accepted for auction. Currently, it sells for approximately $10,000.

Look For

- Examples by silversmiths of renown
- Stylistically extreme toast racks (Art
- Deco spires and geometry, Adamesque ovals, and so on)
- Early nineteenth-century American toast racks, which are extremely rare
- Racks with accessories, such as egg cups or salt and pepper shakers
- And if you're actually planning to use it for toast, that spirit lamp will be helpful.

Stay Away From

- Ostensibly American toast racks with smudgy-looking silver marks. These are highly collectible and often faked. And because there is so little room to stamp marks on such narrow silver, be aware of the fact that both English and American marks are often incomplete.
- Run-of-the-mill designs, especially in twentieth-century toast racks
- Missing or extensively worn ball feet
- Overpolished pieces (any raised detailing will be indistinct)
- Unmarked pieces

Q & A

Why would they want cold toast?
Perhaps they didn't after all. When, in the late eighteenth century, silver toast racks first appeared in England, they were the plain, six-slice model with the little handle that we know today. But by the end of the Georgian era, manufacturers were experimenting with little stands containing spirit lamps to keep things, um, toasty.

Are they always made of silver?
Actually, they're often made in silver plate, which looks like silver.

How can I tell the sterling toast rack from the one that's only silver plated?
English silver hallmarks comprise four separate stamped impressions, usually placed in some unobtrusive spot, such as beneath the object. One of these marks, known as the lion passant, guarantees that the silver content is no less than 92.5 percent; one is the date letter; the third is the mark of the initials of the craftsman; and the last is the town in which the silver was assayed. Silver plate is sometimes marked "silver plate" or "EPNS," for electroplated nickel silver, but often it has imitation "silver" marks. Pieces of American sterling silver will be stamped with the word "sterling."

But if I can't look up the mark while I'm standing in a shop or at an antiques show, how do I judge the age?
The best way is to determine the style. For example, heavy moldings around the base usually mean the piece was made around 1820, while earlier examples can be very delicate. Toast racks followed the fashion for silver in general, so if you've trained your eye to recognize a neoclassical teapot, for instance, or a Victorian rococo revival teapot, then you'll recognize the same aesthetic in the toast rack.

Cameo Glass

Size counts in cameo glass. This Galle example is 14½ inches, but the factory is known for its exceptionally large pieces.

Imagery should reflect the era in which a given piece was made. This mold-blown and etched vase, from 1924, was manufactured at the height of the Art Deco era, and has an appropriately fashionable subject.

Many cameo glass floral and landscape designs are in completely imaginary colors.

Signatures are important to collectors.

Mold blown and etched, this vase is signed in intaglio "Galle."

A Little Backstory

To a piece of brilliantly colored or clear glass, add an "overcoat" of glass in a second color. Then carve your designs in that outer layer, partially removing it to subtly shade or completely expose the base color. That's the basic recipe for cameo glass, a technique known in ancient Rome and repopularized in the late nineteenth century. England, France, and America all produced cameo glass, but probably the best known and most collectible pieces come from Thomas Webb & Sons in England, and Galle, in France.

Q & A

Is it hard to tell real cameo glass from painted glass?
If you run your fingers over each, the cameo glass pattern will feel distinctly raised, or "in relief." Thickly applied paint can feel raised, but it almost never has the crisp edges and tactile topography of carved glass.

The designs are so elaborate. Are they usually floral?
Most often, yes, because most of this glass was made in the Victorian era, after all. But some of the more sophisticated British manufacturers also did classical figures—robed maidens and less-robed heroes, and so forth—and these are quite rare.

Are there other rarities?
The use of three or more colors is unusual, and therefore more valuable than the plain old blue-with-white cameo glass, for instance. White was often used as the topmost color.

And what about signatures?
Galle and Daum Nancy (another French manufacturer) frequently "wrote" their names right on the body of the glass, the way an artist signs a painting. Webb glass is not always signed, although some of the better-known carvers did add their names to pieces that, one assumes, they were particularly pleased with.

Look For
- Signed pieces
- Unusually large pieces
- Cameo glass with figures (usually nymphlike women)
- Glass that combines three colors or more
- Elegant matching of the design to the basic shape of the glass

Stay Away From
- Ground-down rims
- Chips, of course, and always, cracks
- Signed Galle reproductions. In other words, copies (or fakes). Since Galle glass first became valuable, in the 60s, unscrupulous copyists have found it profitable.
- Imitation cameo glass, made in the same time period as the McCoy, but "cut-back" using acid, instead of being hand-carved on a wheel. This was a much less costly method of manufacture. If you look closely, you'll find no subtle shadings in the top coat.

Good This brand-new, 8¾-inch cameo glass vase could fool you. That lavender nasturtium is a pure Art Nouveau design, and it looks to be nicely executed too (lasers?). But the frosted white background, the lack of detail in the "carving," and the unfinished look at the mouth of the vase should put you off. The $100 it sold for may have been too much for a half-baked modern copy of an antique.

Better This 8½-inch vase looks like cameo glass and *is* cameo glass, but it's Chinese, and isn't as collectible as Western examples. How can you tell? It will often have an allover branchy design, and the carving of flowers and fauna will be ill defined and almost clumsily executed. The somewhat unusual colors of this vase helped it to sell for $400.

Best An unusual shape for a cameo glass vase by the famous English manufacturer Thomas Webb & Sons (although not labeled—many aren't), this red 10½-inch vase is carved with exotic flowers and leaves. The work of a master craftsman, it brought $29,000.

Twentieth-Century Silver Plate

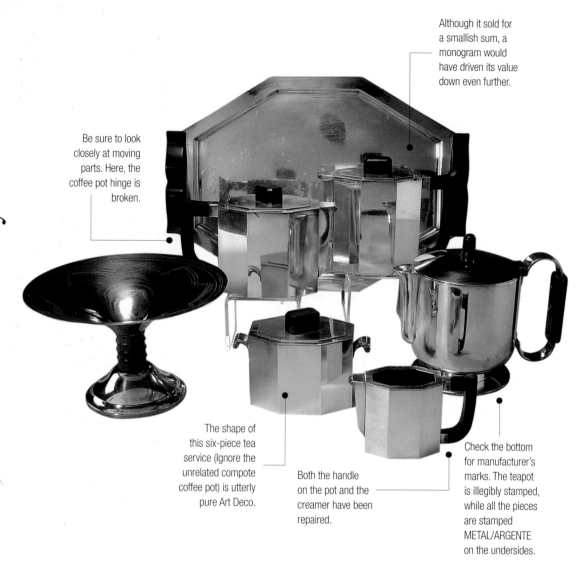

Although it sold for a smallish sum, a monogram would have driven its value down even further.

Be sure to look closely at moving parts. Here, the coffee pot hinge is broken.

The shape of this six-piece tea service (Ignore the unrelated compote coffee pot) is utterly pure Art Deco.

Both the handle on the pot and the creamer have been repaired.

Check the bottom for manufacturer's marks. The teapot is illegibly stamped, while all the pieces are stamped METAL/ARGENTE on the undersides.

A Little Backstory

The most notable difference between modern silver plate and antique silver plate is this: The former is coated with silver by an electroplating process while the designs, for the most part, reflect twentieth-century styles. The examples that are most collectible, in fact, are those that look most modern. But it's important to know that almost no one wants silver plate anymore—antique or modern. After all, if even sterling silver goes begging today (and it does), who wants a recent imitation of silver?

Q & A

How do I tell silver plate from silver?

On antique pieces, look for seams on handles, for a single small hallmark in the shape of a bell, perhaps, or a hand, and a fine silver "wire" beneath the edges, that is the edge of the rolled over silver that hides the copper edge. On modern plate "EPNS" is always a giveaway (it stands for electroplated nickel silver) or, of course, the words "silver plate." Both old and new plated wares tarnish to a kind of irridescent gunmetal (silver doesn't), and on both, the base metal can show through the high spots.

Why does so much silver plate have hallmarks?

Mainly because sterling silver was hallmarked, and makers hoped to borrow some of that credibility. In England, early Sheffield plate wasn't allowed to imitate silver four hallmarks, so early makers used a single personal stamp. (Although much fine old plate has no marks at all. Later on, a plethora of marks on the back that looked something like hallmarks lent both credibility and the possibility of confusion with McCoy.)

Does country of origin matter in silver plate?

Because it was "invented" and flourished in England, most collectors of silver plate look for English wares. Tiffany and Gorham in the United States both made plated silver, but it's not much collected. Other countries are interesting only insofar as their designs are popular.

Look For

- Small, single maker's marks
- High style twentieth-century pieces
- Cocktail shakers from the 1920s, 1930s, and 1940s
- Old Christofle and Odiot plate, both French

Stay Away From

- Overpolished pieces
- Replated pieces. Silver plate loses all its collectible value when it's replated.
- Pieces wrapped with rubber bands or cling wrap, both of which leave ineradicable marks
- Tea sets, the dodo birds of silver plate
- Monogrammed plate (unless it's your own)

Good Probably from the 1940s, but unmarked, this calla lily–form table lamp and its accompanying pair of stork candlesticks are slightly Moderne in style, but not Moderne enough to bring more than $360 for all.

Better This three-piece tea set by Italian tableware designer Lino Sabattini is very small (the teapot is only 7½ inches high), but its design captures the essence of Midcentury Modern. A Ferrari of silver-plated tea sets, it sold for $800.

Best Of silver-plated nickel silver (which would tarnish if unplated), this set of 1905 bottle stoppers in their holder is stamped by Josef Hoffmann, the famed Austrian architect and designer, and Philip Häusler, who worked with Hoffmann at the Weiner Werkstätte in Vienna. Spectacularly contemporary in design, this 4-inch high, 14-inch wide bar accessory was estimated to bring $8,000 to $12,000, but (perhaps because of its highly superfluous function) it didn't find a buyer.

Eighteenth-Century European Dolls

Original mohair wig.

Eyes should be of black glass, without pupils (although late-eighteenth-century dolls may have blue eyes with black pupils).

Pink cheeks are more typical of the earlier dolls; later ones had red cheeks.

The less flaking paint, the better.

Is the style of the dress appropriate to the dolls, and does it show some age?

Is the body all wood, or as here, wood to the waist, with cloth appendages?

A Little Backstory

Dolls are as old as civilization, but those that have been truly loved no longer exist. That's why very few eighteenth-century American dolls have come down to us. In Europe, however, early dolls are found much more frequently. Wooden dolls were the most common (and sturdiest) type, and an English museum, in fact, has a doll that was dressed by Marie Antoinette as she awaited execution. Dolls with happier histories are out there.

Q & A

How were wooden dolls created?

Many were created by doting fathers working on a lathe, turning the doll's head and body in a single piece. Chair makers made dolls and sold them as well, and these can be beautifully carved. The wooden arms were often attached to the torso with leather straps to facilitate movement. Peg woodens or penny woodens have painted heads, bodices, hands and feet—just the parts that showed.

Are these old dolls the ones that are called Queen Anne dolls?

Yes, they are, but the name is misleading, since the Queen's reign ended in 1714, and the dolls in question were made throughout the eighteenth century.

Is condition important?

Collectors don't really expect to find perfection in very early dolls, certainly not the kind of perfection they expect from Barbie (that is, in mint condition in her original box). They make many allowances for the wear and tear of two or three hundred years.

Look For

- Really early dolls, such as those from the seventeenth century. Because there are so few of these, they can easily bring over $20,000.
- Wooden dolls made before 1780
- Dolls made after 1780, which are not as well made as the older models
- Original clothes
- Large dolls
- Dolls with a provenance

Stay Away From

- Wooden dolls that are too perfect, a condition that generally suggests repair
- Orphan dolls; that is, those with no family history
- Really poor condition
- Dolls with the wrong body shape for the era. The eighteenth-century doll has a tapering waist and a long neck. Hands were often forked.

Good Made circa 1750 in England, this 17-inch Queen Anne doll has the requisite long neck and dark glass eyes. Her kid body has wooden limbs, and while her hair and dress are appropriate, they are probably not original. Because her eye and nose are damaged and there is repair around an eye, not to mention patches on her body and new feet, she sold for $1,000!

Better An early English wooden doll, this 15-inch example wears a replacement wig and has tenon-jointed legs articulated at the knees and hip. She's wearing her original shoes and cotton underwear, but sadly, her face and torso have been repainted. She sold for $2,115.

Best Descended in the family of a British peer, this 1775 doll has unquestionable (and impeccable) provenance. She was so well cared for that she's still wearing her original dress, shoes, and underwear. Her bonnet, however, was added around 1800. With only a small flake on her chin (the flake is available to the purchaser!), she sold for $15,209.

Continental Empire Tables

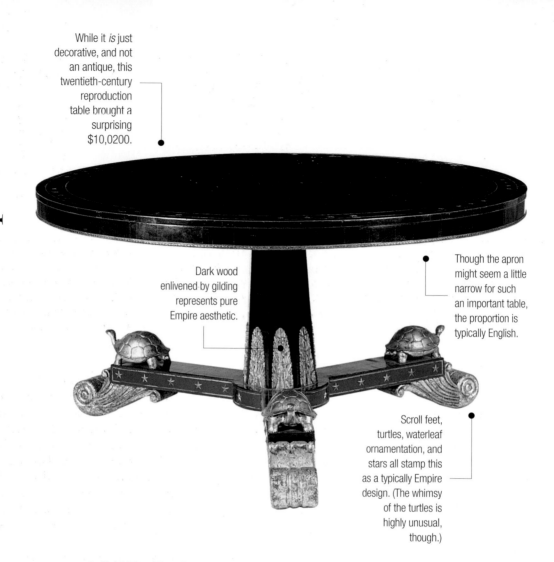

While it *is* just decorative, and not an antique, this twentieth-century reproduction table brought a surprising $10,0200.

Dark wood enlivened by gilding represents pure Empire aesthetic.

Though the apron might seem a little narrow for such an important table, the proportion is typically English.

Scroll feet, turtles, waterleaf ornamentation, and stars all stamp this as a typically Empire design. (The whimsy of the turtles is highly unusual, though.)

A Little Backstory

Late neoclassicism began around the turn of the nineteenth century, just as Napoléon was sweeping all of Europe before him. Simultaneously, Napoleonic wreaths, bees, eagles, medallions, stars, and spears swept through Europe's living rooms, where they also served to complement the newly classical architecture, and even the Russians—nemeses of Napoléon's France—created glorious Empire furniture.

A fixture in drawing rooms of that period, the center table was both a focal point and showpiece. It was also the hub of family gatherings, reading, and games, and most—but not all examples— are round.

Good A nice but unassuming European center table, this piece is second-quarter nineteenth-century French. Its mahogany veneers, metal mounts, and marble top, however, are ordinary and it sold for $1,375.

Better This Italian mahogany and ebonized table—with its inlaid top and Greekish-Roman supports—has a replaced central stem. But designers (as opposed to collectors) don't mind such things, and it brought $12,000.

Best Not pedestal-form, but Empire in design and interesting for the fact that it's an exact copy of a table originally at Fontainebleau, made in the twentieth century by the renowned French cabinetmaker François Linke. Although a reproduction as a double document, it brought $57,600.

Look For

- Tripod bases
- Giltwood elements
- Gilt-bronze ornamentation, used sparingly
- Grandiosity (as long as it's not on a reproduction) is a plus!
- Figural supports
- Makers' signatures in ink, on a paper label, impressed or branded, on the underside

Stay Away From

- Thin marble, usually the sign of a replacement marble top
- Thin veneer, always a mark of a later reproduction
- Late nineteenth-century reproductions. These are very well made and often good copies, but see above.
- Exposed woodworm tunnels on the surface of the wood. Worms don't tunnel on the wooden surface. The tunnels are inside. Put a pin into the worm exit hole. It shouldn't go straight in. Larvae meander. And by the way, American pieces generally don't have wormholes.

Q & A

Is it easy to tell the European or English table from the American table?
Look for light woods, which were popular in Europe, where both wood and marble tops might also be inlaid. In England, pedestal tables were made primarily in mahogany and rosewood, while in France, and some other countries, oak was used as a secondary wood. American pieces use pine as a secondary wood. (Examine those hidden parts with a flashlight to be sure.)

In England, the Empire style was known as Regency, and on the whole, English Regency tables are less flamboyant than those of European origin. They often seem more architectural too (especially pieces modeled after designs by craftsmen Thomas Hope and, to a lesser extent, George Smith).

If I buy an Empire period table made on the Continent, does it matter which country it came from?
It doesn't matter as much to Americans as it does to Italians, say, or the Spanish, who like to own their own history, just as many of us do. What matters most when buying these tables is their age and authenticity. (And don't forget that Austria, Sweden, Belgium, Russia, Germany, and Italy all had tables too. Everything European isn't French, by a long shot.)

What exactly is Biedermeier? It looks classical-Regency-Empire too.
It's the northern European version of Empire, popular from about 1815 to 1850. Instead of having gilt, stenciled, or bronze ornamentation, it's very simple, all about line and matched veneers on beautifully grained pale woods like maple, ash, and fruitwoods. Biedermeier is often trimmed in ebony. Its simplicity may reflect a reaction to the pomposity of the French Napoleonic style.

Teapots

The lid should fit perfectly.

A fancy finial would be a plus. Check for reglued breaks at the neck.

The shiny glaze—the glassy coating that covers the ceramic—keeps it from absorbing liquids.

Feel around the tip of the spout for chips.

Watch out. Handles are often broken and repaired.

It looks like majolica, but this cauliflower pot is eighteenth-century English pottery!

Animal-, vegetable-, and even the occasional mineral-shaped teapot is especially collectible.

A mark on the bottom of the pot might tell you the age, country of origin, or the maker.

The foot ring shouldn't be chipped or cracked.

A Little Backstory

The drinking of tea was to the eighteenth century what latte drinking is today, but you don't have to be a tea drinker to love a teapot. In the twenty-first century, they're popular collectibles, since what else has such an appealing shape, takes up so little houseroom, is both dignified and down-home, and functional to boot? There's a huge and varied market for teapots too, so you'll find lots to choose from.

Good This little pot, marked "Japan," is made of indistinctly detailed white pottery trimmed haphazardly in gold paint. But it's decorated with a colorful printed (not hand-painted) bouquet, and is worth every penny of its $10 price tag.

Better (especially in England) From the 1931 tableware line of British pottery designer Clarice Cliff comes a quintessentially Art Deco teapot (the shape is Stamford), the pattern House and Bridge. This humble collectible is worth $1,700.

Best How can this Chinese porcelain teapot with its cracked spout—only 6 inches tall and 180 years old (in China that's new)—be worth $21,000? It was made for the imperial household: Rarity—and emperors—trump damage.

Look For

- Unusual shapes from all eras, especially the 1930s
- Until the late eighteenth century, tea was quite expensive and was served in little pots, so very small porcelain teapots can sometimes be very old.
- Rarity of decoration or shape, because generally speaking, the more of one teapot that's out there, the less valuable it's likely to be.

Stay Away From

- Limited editions, especially those that come with "certificates of authenticity." They'll go the way of Beanie Babies, but will need to be dusted more often.
- Until you really know your field, avoid any teapot that's high priced enough to keep you awake at night.
- Damage of any kind. Teapot collectors are pretty unforgiving.

Q & A

How can I tell if a teapot is old?
Teapots made before 1905 (or basically, one hundred years ago from the current date) are legally antiques. "Vintage" pieces tend to be not much older than your grandmother (and sometimes, your mother), while contemporary teapots can be younger than you are.

Pots marked with the name of the country of origin (Japan, for example, or Czechoslovakia or England) are always made after 1893. Unmarked pieces may or may not be older. The easiest way to find out is to compare their shapes to drawings or pictures in books on ceramics (see opposite).

Is the oldest teapot usually the most valuable one?
Not anymore. In fact, in today's market, a Mickey Mouse teapot from the 1940s can easily be pricier than a Victorian pot of hand-painted Royal Worcester.

Where can I go to compare the interesting mark I've found on the bottom of my teapot to other marks?
There are so many good, well-illustrated books on marks. On the Web, the New York Public Library has an easy-to-use site, as does a by-subscription service called ceramicmarksfinder.com.

If the mark I'm researching does match a mark in a book, how would I know if my piece is fake or not?
Unless your teapot has an eighteenth-century maker's mark, it's actually not likely to be fake—mainly because ceramic teapots haven't been collectible or high priced long enough to make them financially worthwhile for fakers to copy.

Weather Vanes

Check seams and
wing tips for repairs.

And just what is
it with farm boys,
weather vanes, and
guns? Too many
gunshot holes, or
filled-in gunshot
holes, affect value
adversely.

$1,500
Look for a label.
If you have
access to original
manufacturers'
catalogues, you can
sometimes make an
attribution. This late-
nineteenth-, early
twentieth-century
hollow-bodied
copper example is
attributed to A. L.
Jewell.

A Little Backstory

What could be more all-American than an eagle weather vane?
There are infinitely more of them than there are locust or
fish weather vanes. And probably a lot more eagles than dogs,
Gabriels, or figures of Liberty. But not all eagles are equal. Some
are more or less heroic than others, and some—lackluster ones—
seem often to lay an auction egg.

Q & A

How were they made?

American weather vanes are sold in Folk Art sales, which means that they're frequently—not always—the work of amateurs who cut them out of sheet tin with shears; sometimes these do-it-yourselfers painted them, as well. But among the most beautiful are the commercially made weather vanes: those three-dimensional beauties sold by companies specializing in the technique of hammering copper over a wood mold. The copper halves were seamed together to make a hollow rooster, a leaping stag, a fish, a fire engine, or an eagle.

Which are most popular?

The best vanes had strong outlines so they could be seen from a distance, but the most artistic vanes convey an exciting sense of windswept movement. Collectors like trotting horses and sulkies, and nobly prancing steeds. Among the costliest weather vanes are those depicting Native Americans.

Are they ever signed?

Some of them, though not all, are labeled by their manufacturers, several of whom specialized in particular designs. The best-known makers are Josiah Harrison, J. W. Fiske, L.W. Cushing and Sons, and Cushing and White. All worked in the Northeast.

Look For

- Attractively weathered vanes
- Supports or braces that are unobtrusive
- Individualistic or eccentric subjects and careful workmanship
- Original paint
- A rich green patina (actually oxidation) on copper weather vanes
- Exceptional size

Stay Away From

- Gold radiator paint instead of original gilding
- New paint. Old paint looks crazed.
- Overly restored or clumsily restored vanes, or those with replaced parts
- Wooden vanes, which haven't held up very well and tend to have little detail
- Fake cut-metal weather vanes

Good This circa 1900 10-inch-tall copper eagle is small and a little too late to be considered Folk Art, and its wing position may not be fierce enough—all of which add up to a $500 selling price.

Better Here's a twentieth-century 28 x 37¼-inch painted eagle cut from a sheet of iron with one wing tip sadly bent. This example looks as if it's been copied from a manufacturer's logo (motor oil? cake flour?). Yet the red paint, chipped though it is, adds considerable zing. It brought $550.

Best This fierce eagle, with its heroically outstretched wings and open beak, is of hollow molded copper, as is the orb that's attached to the copper arrow. All elements have wonderful detail and an excellent green patina that retains traces of original gilding. This large weather vane (37 × 71 inches) sold for $42,000.

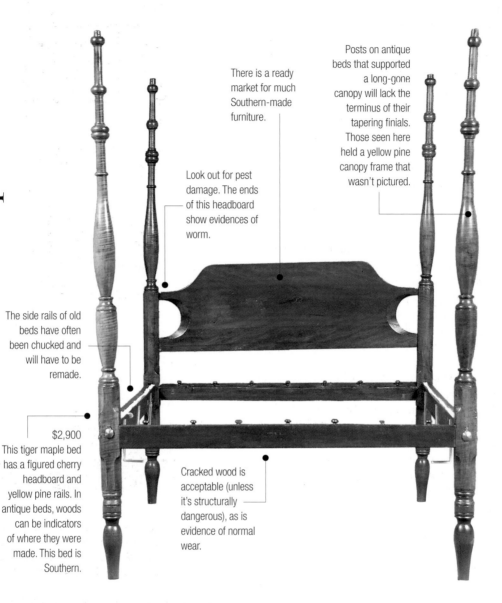

Four-poster Beds

There is a ready market for much Southern-made furniture.

Posts on antique beds that supported a long-gone canopy will lack the terminus of their tapering finials. Those seen here held a yellow pine canopy frame that wasn't pictured.

Look out for pest damage. The ends of this headboard show evidences of worm.

The side rails of old beds have often been chucked and will have to be remade.

$2,900
This tiger maple bed has a figured cherry headboard and yellow pine rails. In antique beds, woods can be indicators of where they were made. This bed is Southern.

Cracked wood is acceptable (unless it's structurally dangerous), as is evidence of normal wear.

A Little Backstory

Shakespeare bequeathed his second-best bed to his wife, but his very best bed was surely a four-poster, one with all the trimmings: goose-down pillows, feather mattresses, heavy bed-hangings to keep out the cold, a "roof" (as the English call a canopy) and in all likelihood, Elizabethan bedbugs. The four-poster style is still popular today, though antique examples are not, even though we can buy them, mostly, without the wildlife.

Q & A

Why is it that four-posters seem so special?
Could it be romance? Or perhaps it's some unconscious remnant of medieval times, when the bed of the highest-ranked member of a household was the only one permitted to have a full canopy. As you descended the family hierarchy, the canopies got smaller.

Am I better off buying an antique bed than a new one?
If you're planning to share your bed with anyone larger than a small dog, no. Antique beds are narrower and sometimes shorter than new ones. And even if you don't mind not being able to roll over during the night, you could find yourself having to buy a custom mattress and custom sheets. On the other hand, older beds are frequently constructed of beautiful woods, or enhanced with fine-quality carvings and inlays. In the 1920s, American manufacturers like Wallace Nutting made excellent copies of Federal-era beds, and (despite the fact that old beds, in general, are fairly hard to sell), these reproductions have become somewhat collectible. Nutting's beds, like the originals they're based on, are only single or double size.

Why do some old beds have really plain headboards?
Generally speaking, that's because the headboard was intended to be hidden behind the bed curtains and pillows. Many American beds had canopies hung with delicate crocheted testers or alternatively, with sets of curtains that kept out drafts, insects, and Sunday-morning children. The need for protection disappeared with the arrival of central heating and air-conditioning.

Look For

- A graceful proportion in post height to bed size
- Decoratively painted four-posters and, always, original paint
- Beautiful quality carving
- On old beds, those side rails that hold front and back together
- Unusual treatment of vertical elements: twists and fluting (scooped-out hollows) or foliate carving

Stay Away From

- Vintage beds with missing finials
- Antique beds that have been widened to accommodate newer mattress sizes
- Refinished old beds. (Take the sniff test. New varnish or lacquer will occasionally still smell.)
- Antique twin beds, which, by the way, *never* came in pairs!

Good A nineteenth-century American mahogany spool-turned four-poster bed is both attractive and genuinely antique. Nevertheless, it's only what used to be called a double size, which isn't what today's buyers want. That's why it brought $120.

Better From its simple headboard to its brass bolt covers, this is a faithful copy of a circa 1800 American bed. This bed is slightly narrower than the "good" example. Nevertheless, it sold for $1,299—more than many a genuine antique bed. Blame it on that curvy canopy.

Best A 1940s queen-size mahogany bed by Tommi Parzinger is severely elegant, (except for its cupped and scalloped—almost floral—flanged finials). Its $20,400 price tag reflects the current interest in designer Midcentury Modern furniture, which *may* hold its value, but *may* turn out to be an overpriced trend.

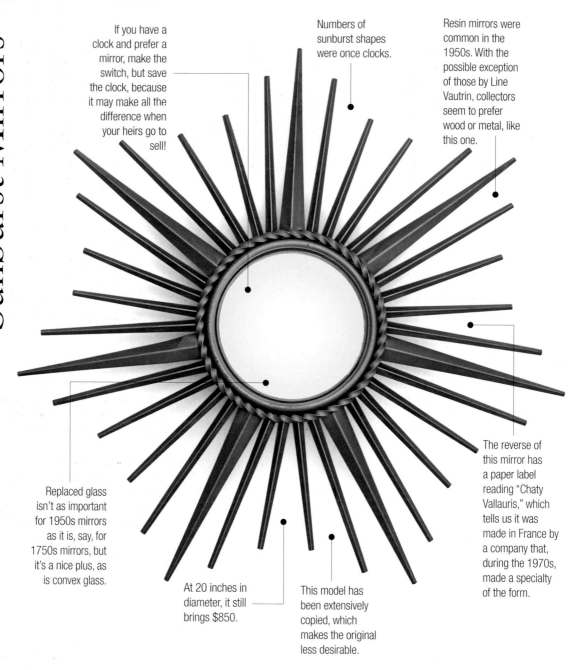

Sunburst Mirrors

If you have a clock and prefer a mirror, make the switch, but save the clock, because it may make all the difference when your heirs go to sell!

Numbers of sunburst shapes were once clocks.

Resin mirrors were common in the 1950s. With the possible exception of those by Line Vautrin, collectors seem to prefer wood or metal, like this one.

Replaced glass isn't as important for 1950s mirrors as it is, say, for 1750s mirrors, but it's a nice plus, as is convex glass.

At 20 inches in diameter, it still brings $850.

This model has been extensively copied, which makes the original less desirable.

The reverse of this mirror has a paper label reading "Chaty Vallauris," which tells us it was made in France by a company that, during the 1970s, made a specialty of the form.

A Little Backstory

Like the sun, sunburst mirrors are currently hot. They haven't been this hot since the 1950s, and after that—pardon the pun— they were pretty much in eclipse. But flaming disks are warming rooms again, filling awkward gaps, combining well with every style, beaming chic, and reflecting joy. Sunscreens aren't required.

Good This carved-wood Italian sunburst of uncertain age, but distinctly Directoire parentage (note the beading around the mirror frame) is exuberantly traditional. With an $800–$1,200 estimate and at around 2 feet in diameter, it's not inexpensive but still a nice buy.

Better Made in France in the late 1940s, the widely spaced, hand-forged iron "flames" of this gilt-finished metal sunburst and its twisted mirror frame are fairly sophisticated. It's a very urban $2,400.

Best A flare in the sunburst firmament was caused by the sale of a spiky resin model named Roi Soleil by the French Line Vautrin. Circa 1960, it sold at auction in 2006 for $168,000, a price having to do with size, condition, or materials, and everything to do with fashion and he artist's name.

Look For

- Oval mirrors, or pairs of mirrors, because both are less common
- Unusual ray arrangements with lots of "air" in between the rays, for instance, or double- and triple-decker rays
- Large examples, which are more expensive
- Mirrors with original old and wavy glass
- "Designer" mirrors. See that shocking "best" above.
- Labeled mirrors

Stay Away From

- Vintage mirror designs that are being copied in current furniture catalogues. Reproductions downgrade the value of the originals.
- Wooden mirrors with "missing teeth." But if they're just loose or leaning a little, they can often be reglued.
- Wooden mirrors that have lost too much gilding (unless you really love shabby)
- Damaged resin mirrors. Among commercially manufactured mirrors, resin is least desirable.

Q & A

Why do you suppose they're popular again?
It's all about the decorators. They've seriously rediscovered the "Hollywood Regency" style, that shiny and glamorous 1940s and 1950s take on English Regency furnishings. Hollywood Regency was a silver screen moment: a little tongue-in-cheek, a little ironic, a little David Niven and a lot of style.

How do I know how old a sunburst mirror is? And does it matter?
Let's be honest, it's hard to really know because there are so many mid-century mirrors, and plenty of those were dirtied-up to look antique. The sunburst shape, which has always been popular since ancient times and may derive, in fact, from church altarpieces. Fortunately, there are examples from the last century that were labeled, while many of the genuinely old ones are in sad but convincing shape because their gold leaf has chipped away to expose the white gessoed wood beneath. Age only matters, really, if one of these mirrors is being offered as antique.

Are there other finishes besides gold leaf?
Metal examples can have brass, silver, and copper finishes or various types of real and artificially blackened iron. Sometimes the "rays" have been stamped with relief patterns, like the ribs of leaves, or there are hand-wrought rims around the mirror.

Are wood sunbursts any better or more expensive than those made of metal?
Not at all. Innumerable iron examples come from countries like Spain, where wrought and forged iron are traditional, while the wood mirrors seem to be more typical of Italy. Unsurprisingly, the form is especially popular in hot countries.

Midcentury Dining Tables

Bold and attractive wood grain is a prerequisite for this type of midcentury furniture.

Special detail adds value. This top is inlaid with various-size silver paillettes.

This leg shape is typical of the period.

Look beneath the top for a label or brand that indicates the maker. Labels change over the years, and that can help in dating a piece.

The designer here has used rosewood.

A Little Backstory

Everyone needs a dining room table—for homework, for wrapping gifts, for eating on—but mainly for matching that set of eight chairs. In the 1950s, everyone seemed to need a "green" table (although it wasn't called that then), preferably one designed in Europe and made of exotic wood—not polished and not carved. Scandinavian design had its finger on the postwar pulse, as it does again on the pulse of collectors today.

Good Designed by Hans Wegner and produced by Andreas Tuck (which dates it after 1950), this 55-inch table with two leaves is branded on the underside. Too plain, too late, or both, it sold for a mere $1,440.

Better This walnut pedestal table, 28 × 42 inches in diameter, is attributed to American George Nakashima. It lacks a label, but has an excellent provenance and sold for $9,000.

Best This unsigned 1951 mahogany dining table by Gio Ponti is 53 x 31 inches and sold for $30,000, accompanied by a letter of authenticity from Ponti's archives.

Look For

- Perfect condition
- A label, or other marking, beneath the top
- Finn Juhl tables designed for Baker
- Any table by Gio Ponti
- Decorator-designed pieces made between the 1920s and the 1960s
- Experimental pieces, which are usually one of a kind

Stay Away From

- Reproductions of midcentury designs. There are still plenty of originals if you want one.
- Badly marred surfaces. Cigarette burns are indigenous to midcentury furniture.
- In the 1950, and 1960s, it was considered "good housekeeping" to oil your Scandinavian furniture. Oil picks up dirt, however, and makes for a lot of sixty-year-old gunk— sometimes known in the antiques world as patina, although I don't know what the vintage furniture people call it. (Check with specialists in vintage for the latest on cleaning tabletops.)
- Tables lacking their original leaves

Q & A

They all look so much alike. How can I tell if I'm looking at a major table or a ho-hum table?

In the current market, it seems to be purely the reputation of the table's maker. If his (or rarely, her) work is in the collections of several good museums, that generally indicates that scholars in this field value the genius of that designer. This—and there being enough of the designer's work available for a market to be made—is how modern furniture becomes collectible. It's all about names.

These pieces must have been much less expensive to make, for instance, than reproductions of Duncan Phyfe. But were they expensive when they were new?

The tables imported from Europe weren't terribly costly in the 1950s. Several Scandinavian lines, however, were sold mainly in specialty stores, and some, then and now, were considerably more expensive than Duncan Phyfe antiques.

They seem so clean and beautifully proportioned just as they are. Do most dining room tables of this era come with extra leaves?

Many more dining tables had leaves than not. Christmas dinners, after all, are served throughout the world.

Are four-legged examples more collectible than pedestal tables?

Not at all. It's purely a matter of taste (although with pedestals, no diner gets stuck with a leg).

Is it important to have the matching chairs?

The idea of a set of dining room furniture is fairly recent. And while it might be nice to have a match, provided the chairs you place around your table are complementary, it's far from a necessity. Nor will that necessarily make one table more valuable than another.

Travel Posters

There should be no visible repairs, although some invisible ones are allowable.

Look out for the brown spots known as foxing on the paper.

Edges shouldn't be torn or tattered, and blobs of old tape at the corners (or anywhere, for that matter) affect value too.

Watch out for faded color. The hues should be as fresh and as bright as the day the poster came off the printing press.

Wrinkles, fold lines, and creases are not only unsightly, they make any poster more fragile and detract from it's value.

It's important that margins (including plain white margins) have not been trimmed and the paper is the size it's supposed to be (see overleaf).

Eye appeal is key to collectibility, and this colorful poster has it all: the pretty woman, the flowers, the azure seas, and the gorgeously romantic landscape.

The early 1920s style of this poster makes it particularly desirable. Collectors prize posters from that era.

The signature identifies the artist, who may or may not be well known. The work of famous artists is usually more valuable.

PARIS - LYON - MÉDITERRANÉE

MONACO MONTE-CARLO AU PAYS DU SOLEIL

A Little Backstory

With a single picture and a few choice words, the best travel posters—big, colorful, razzmatazz ads—persuaded the public to get up and *go!* Old examples, from the late nineteenth and early twentieth century, were lithographs, while later posters might be photo-offset; but *all* were multiples, which means that hundreds, even thousands, of copies were originally made of each. Considering this, it's utterly amazing that given their hard, short lives on lamp poles and billboards, there are still so many left to buy.

Good This somewhat surreal 1950s poster—published by the Spanish State Tourist Department—is eye-catching, but because we don't know its artist, and its subject doesn't excite collectors, it's worth just $325.

Better Printed in Hanoi, this 1931 poster is visually arresting and rare. Few from Indochina remain, and this one has not only faded, it also has repaired tears through the margins and right into the text and image. Nevertheless, $2,300 is fair.

Best With all the advantages of the *Monaco* poster (pretty girl, wonderful color, and so forth), this 1935 beauty has one further advantage: It's an American subject. We love American subjects. Its $10,000 price tag would have bought quite a few trips to Atlantic City.

Look For

- Ocean liner and railway posters from 1900 to 1950. Great transatlantic ships and glamorous train travel pretty much disappeared after that, and collectors are nostalgic
- Posters with original margins: those that haven't been trimmed to fit someone's picture frame. (You can find the original size of many posters in auction catalogues or on the Web.)
- French Art Deco posters from the 1920s, which are scarce as Gauloises, but equally breathtaking.
- Posters for the return trip of the *Titanic.* (Yes, there is one!)

Stay Away From

- Reproductions of famous poster images. (Reproductions won't delight your heirs, because none are valuable. The International Vintage Poster Dealers Association lists known reproductions.)
- Posters that have been glued down to cardboard backings
- Somber posters (unless they have personal significance)

Q & A

Some lithographed posters sell for thousands. How do I know if I'm looking at an old one or a worthless reproduction?
The quickest—but definitely not the only—way is to check the paper it's printed on. Antique posters (those famous ones by Toulouse-Lautrec, for instance) were printed on porous, newspaper-like paper; *never* on glossy paper.

What if it's covered by glass?
Examine the colored image through a magnifying glass. You can easily see if it's made up of tiny dots (like those in comic books) and if it is, you're looking at a photographic reproduction, not a lithograph.

If there are so many of the same poster out there, how can I possibly know if mine is one of the better ones?
If your poster is signed, and many are, you can Google the artist's name and find out if he's famous; punchy subjects are good too—strong images of planes, for instance—or trains, cars, or the golden beaches of Capri; rarity is crucial, but tricky, because we don't always know how many were produced; and beauty is, well, in the eye of the beholder. Finally, there's condition.

Is condition important?
So important that experts use grades. An A poster has fresh colors and no big tears, though *small* blemishes are permissible. The B poster can have invisibly repaired tears or invisible repainting, with minimal fading or discoloring, while the C poster might have any or all of the above, but way too much of it. (Run your hand over the paper, if it's not under glass, to feel for repainting or repairs.)

Eighteenth-Century Continental Porcelain Figures

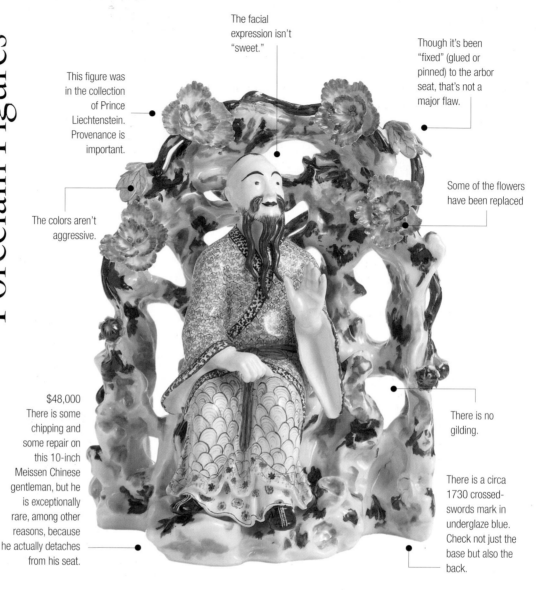

This figure was in the collection of Prince Liechtenstein. Provenance is important.

The facial expression isn't "sweet."

Though it's been "fixed" (glued or pinned) to the arbor seat, that's not a major flaw.

The colors aren't aggressive.

Some of the flowers have been replaced

$48,000 There is some chipping and some repair on this 10-inch Meissen Chinese gentleman, but he is exceptionally rare, among other reasons, because he actually detaches from his seat.

There is no gilding.

There is a circa 1730 crossed-swords mark in underglaze blue. Check not just the base but also the back.

A Little Back Story

There was a time, not all that long ago, when sophisticated collectors' cabinets were full of eighteenth-century Continental porcelains. The figures they sought out were cunningly made, with detail and freshness of color that's jaw dropping. These earliest examples of the European discovery of porcelain have become so rare and costly, however, that the average buyer is pretty much shut out of the market. But, then, they were luxury products when new, so maybe it's no wonder they are today. Sour grapes, perhaps, but they *are* a problem to dust.

Q & A

Why do so many of these figures seem to be backed by a tree trunk or arbor?

That arbor is called a *bocage,* which is French for foliage. Its purpose, along with being a pretty appendage, is to support the "freestanding" porcelain figures. Otherwise, they might collapse while being fired in the kiln.

What's the difference between Meissen and Dresden?

In the very early eighteenth century, the Meissen factory (in Meissen, Germany) became the first in Europe to discover the elusive formula for hard-paste porcelain, and Meissen, with its royal backing, became the standard against which all European porcelain was judged. Years later, in the 1840s, the company enjoyed great success by reissuing its own early wares (see Nineteenth-Century Continental Porcelain). Smaller factories in nearby Dresden copied Meissen's crossed-swords mark and produced their own, occasionally overdecorated, figures.

And what's the difference between Meissen and Sèvres?

They were the two most important eighteenth-century producers of porcelain. When, from 1756 to 1763, Meissen's output was seriously affected by the Seven Years' War, the royally protected French factory at Vincennes (which later became Sèvres) supplanted it. Sèvres produced graceful, typically French figures. Later, when Neoclassical became the rage, it turned to restrained figures in biscuit.

Look For

- Soft-paste porcelain, which almost always has imperfections both in the shape (usually a little "off") and in the white body (look for small black specks)
- Rare subjects (although here in America, we're lucky to find any figures at all, except at major auctions)
- Pieces that seem understated, not decorated with lots of gilding, color, and fussiness. Those are likely to be fakes.

Stay Away From

- Copies by Samson, a well-known nineteenth-century maker of porcelain reproductions (now collectible themselves!)
- Soft-paste marks on hard-paste porcelain (check those books on marks)
- Brown spots, which *can* indicate age, but not necessarily
- Damaged pieces
- Look for repairs by feeling the piece all over for textural anomalies and checking to see that there are no matte spots on shiny areas, the sign of imperfectly executed repairs.
- Regilded edges and highlights. Golds are especially difficult to match.

Good Despite having a repaired base, an unmarked 7-inch figure of a smiling boy offering an owl for sale, made by one of the lesser French factories (either Niderviller or Luneville) brought $1,700 at auction.

Better This circa 1750, 9½-inch figure, modeled by Kaendler, Meissen's great modeler, depicts Calliope, goddess of epic poetry. She seems, here, to be composing. The tree beneath which she sits has been restored, as have the leaves on the base. A firing crack (a flaw occurring in the kiln) at the base may have affected her selling price, for this figure brought only $6,000. Fire cracks, by the way, are always random, never a straight line.

Best A Niderviller shepherd and shepherdess are 2 inches tall and are unpainted (i.e., bisque). Every detail is crisp, they are a pair (always more valuable), and they are both unrestored. Created within the last fifteen years of the eighteenth century, this elegant and fairly large couple sold for $31,000.

Wineglasses

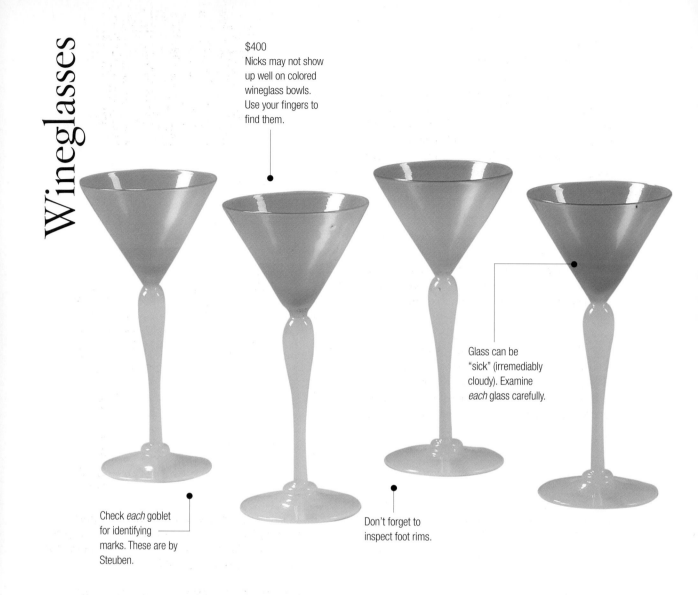

$400
Nicks may not show up well on colored wineglass bowls. Use your fingers to find them.

Glass can be "sick" (irremediably cloudy). Examine *each* glass carefully.

Check *each* goblet for identifying marks. These are by Steuben.

Don't forget to inspect foot rims.

A Little Backstory

Art glass epitomizes a fragile, hand-wrought moment in nineteenth- and early twentieth-century decorative arts. It started with genius Louis Comfort Tiffany's attempts to copy ancient Roman glass, and ended with scores of other companies copying—with varying degrees of aptitude—his success. Among the best of his competitors was Steuben.

Q & A

If I have only eleven Tiffany wineglasses left of my great-grandmother's set of twelve, does that hurt the value of the set?
If your great grandmother's set were just pretty glass, having just eleven *would* be a drawback. But even single pieces of stemware are sold at auction when their maker is as popular as Tiffany. This is seldom the case with other types of stemware, though, except perhaps for seventeenth-century English drinking glasses, rare early Venetian glasses, and certain Art Nouveau and Art Deco wares.

What about damage?
Glass collectors are notoriously finicky, and with the exception of very ancient glass and, again, the earliest Venetian glass, they won't accept any damage at all. Basically, the closer an item is to having been made to our own time, the more they expect perfection.

And what about signatures and marks?
Again, because we're usually dealing with fairly recent items that were usually marked by their manufacturers—either with an etched or scratched-in mark, a relief-molded mark, a paper label, or any of these in combination—collectors have learned to prefer those with unequivocal, legible signatures.

Look For

- Unusual colors for a given factory
- Oversize examples
- Paper labels, because they've so often been washed off
- Faintly scratched-in signatures, which may be hidden among the scratches caused by years of use
- The sinuous, naturalistic shapes that characterize the Art Nouveau era

Stay Away From

- Mended glass. Run your finger around the top to discover the slight unevenness indicating that a chip has been ground down.
- Do the same with the foot rim.
- Hold the glass up to the light, to be certain the stem isn't broken and glued back together.
- Flashed glass, resembling colored glass, but with its color *applied* to the surface. (This can often be scratched off with a fingernail.)

Good The blue is quite an attractive color on this group of glasses by Steuben, each 8½ inches high, with threading applied on the exterior. Signed on the bottom and in overall good condition, this set of wineglasses brought $2,000.

Better It could be argued that these "marriage goblet" wineglasses are no better than the ones above. They're clear glass—more common than colored glass—and while they are signed Steuben, there are only two, and why would anyone buy just two glasses for $518? Perhaps because they're 12 inches tall and were in the Woolworth Collection. (Or perhaps their buyer needed a wedding gift.)

Best This enamel decorated wineglass from the palace of Nicholas II, etched on the underside with the imperial mark and the date, 1915, is only 6¹/₈ inches high, and not, of itself, a superb example of the glassmaker's art. Nevertheless, it brought $5,000, because relics from the court of the last Russian czar are both rare and highly sought after.

Acknowledgments

My thanks to . . .

First and foremost, David Murphy—a man of infinite good humor, dependability, patience, versatility, and, luckily, an extreme tolerance of pizza.

Megan Newman, for her confidence in this book and her admirable forbearance and for making this process so pleasant.

Miriam Rich, for her helpfulness and her amazing efficiency in the face of endless data, queries, and complexities.

Stephen Drucker, a fine editor and a treasured friend.

Matthew Weigman at Sotheby's, for his (very) long-distance and highly valuable assistance.

Jeni L. Sandberg at Christies, who never minds passing on bits of her comprehensive and ever-expanding knowledge.

Monica Reuss at Northeast, for assistance above and beyond the call of duty (and her somehow comforting weather reports from New Hampshire).

Anne Trodella at Skinner, who provided swift, capable, and excellent responses to the smallest query.

The "girlfriends," Clare Potter and Deborah Webster, my Sunday-night support group.

All the unknown researchers at every auction house that generously allowed us the use of hundreds of perfect images for this book.

Richard and Judy Lincoff . . . my favorite relatives and moral supporters.

Carolan Workman, my ultimate stress reliever. Pink card not required.

Tucker Velocity Prisant—sweet, kind, beautiful, and smart. (She writes Good stories, too, that every day get Better.)

Barden and Catherine Prisant—Always the Best.

Resources

Adam A. Weschler & Son, Inc.
909 E Street, N.W.
Washington, D.C. 20004
Tel: (202) 628-1281
www.weschlers.com

Brunk Auctions
P.O. Box 2135
Asheville, NC 28802
Tel: (828) 254-6846
www.brunkauctions.com

Charlton Hall Galleries, Inc.
912 Gervais Street
Columbia, SC 29201
Tel: (803) 779-5678
www.charltonhallauctions.com

Christie's
20 Rockefeller Plaza
6
New York, NY 10020
Tel: (212) 636-2000
www.Christies.com
(other locations worldwide)

The Cobbs Auctioneers
50 Jaffrey Road
Peterborough, NH 03458
Tel: (603) 924-6361
www.thecobbs.com

Cowan's Auctions
6270 Este Avenue
Cincinnati, OH 45232
Tel: (513) 871-1670
www.cowans.com

Dan Ripley's Antique Helper Auctions
2764 E 55th Place
Indianapolis, IN 46220
Tel: (317) 251-5635
www.antiquehelper.com

Dawson & Nye
128 The American Road
Morris Plains, NJ 07950
Tel: (973) 984-6900
www.dawsonandnye.com

Doyle New York
175 East 87th Street
New York, NY 10128
Tel: (212) 427-2730
www.doylenewyork.com

DuMouchelles Art Gallery
409 East Jefferson Avenue
Detroit, MI 48226
Tel: (313) 963-6255
www.dumouchelle.com

Early American
P.O. Box 3507
Rancho Santa Fe, CA 92067
Tel: (858) 759-3290
www.earlyamerican.com

James D. Julia Auctioneers
P.O. Box 830
203 Skowhegan Road
Fairfield, ME 04937
Tel: (207) 453-7125
www.jamesdjulia.com

Leslie Hindman Auctioneers
1338 West Lake Street
Chicago, IL 60607
Tel: (312) 280-1212
www.lesliehindman.com

Neal Auction Company
4038 Magazine Street
New Orleans, LA 70115
Tel: (504) 899-5329
www.nealauction.com

Noel Barrett
P.O. Box 300
Carversville, PA 18913
Tel: (215) 297-5109
www.noelbarrett.com

Northeast Auctions
93 Pleasant Street
Portsmouth, NH 03801
Tel: (603) 433-8400
www.northeastauctions.com

Pook & Pook, Inc.
463 East Lancaster Avenue
Downingtown, PA 19336
Tel: (610) 269-4040
www.pookandpook.com

Rago Arts and Auction Center
333 North Main Street
Lambertville, NJ 08530
Tel: (609) 397-9374
www.ragoarts.com

Samuel T. Freeman & Co.
1808 Chestnut Street
Philadelphia, PA 19103
Tel: (215) 563-9275
www.freemansauction.com

Sanford Alderfer Auction & Appraisal
501 Fairgrounds Road
Hatfield, PA 19440
Tel: (215) 393-3000
www.alderferauction.com

Skinner, Inc. Auctioneers and
    Appraisers of Antiques and Fine Art
63 Park Plaza
Boston, MA 02116
Tel: (617) 350-5400

and

274 Cedar Hill Street
Marlborough, MA 01752
Tel: (508) 970-3000
www.skinnerinc.com

Sloans & Kenyon
7034 Wisconsin Avenue
Chevy Chase, MD 20815
Tel: (301) 634-2330
www.sloansandkenyon.com

Sotheby's Auction House
1334 York Avenue at 72nd Street
New York, NY 10021
Tel: (212) 606-7000
www.sothebys.com
(other locations worldwide)

Thomaston Place Auction Galleries
51 Atlantic Highway, US Rt. 1
Thomaston, ME 04861
Tel: (207) 354-8141
www.thomastonauction.com

Waddington's
111 Bathurst Street
Toronto, Ontario
Canada M5V 2R1
Tel: 001-416-504-5100
www.wadingtons.ca

Wright
1440 West Hubbard
Chicago, IL 60622
Tel: (312) 563-0020
www.wright20.com

Credits

1. *Nineteenth-century enameled glass*
   Hero and Better photos courtesy of Skinner, Boston and Marlborough, MA
   Good photo courtesy of Pook & Pook, Inc., Downingtown, PA
   Best photo © Leslie Hindman Auctioneers, Inc., 2006, Chicago, IL

2. *Midcentury dining chairs*
   Hero, Good, Better, and Best photos courtesy of Wright, Chicago, IL

3. *Oriental rugs*
   Hero photo courtesy of Sotheby's
   Good photo courtesy of The Cobbs Auctioneers, Peterborough, NH
   Better photo courtesy of Charlton Hall Galleries, Inc., Columbia, SC
   Best photo courtesy of Northeast Auctions, Portsmouth, NH

4. *Cat paintings*
   Hero photo © Christie's Images Limited
   Good, Better, and Best photos reprinted by permission from *House Beautiful*, Hearst Communications, Inc.

5. *American tea tables*
   Hero and Better photos courtesy of Neal Auction Company, New Orleans, LA
   Good photo courtesy of Sloans & Kenyon Auctioneers and Appraisers, Chevy Chase, MD
   Best photo courtesy of Sotheby's

6. *Silver cream pitchers*
   Hero photo courtesy of Sotheby's
   Good and Best photos © Christie's Images Limited
   Better photo courtesy of Rago Arts and Auction Center, Lambertville, NJ

7. *Doorstops*
   Hero, Good, Better, and Best photos reprinted by permission from *House Beautiful*, Hearst Communications, Inc.

8. *American neoclassical (empire) center tables*
   Hero photo courtesy of Northeast Auctions, Portsmouth, NH
   Good photo courtesy of Waddington's, Toronto, Ontario, Canada
   Better photo courtesy of Neal Auction Co., New Orleans, LA
   Best photo courtesy of Sotheby's

9. *Parian*
   Hero and Better photos courtesy of Rago Arts and Auction Center, Lambertville, NJ
   Good and Best photos courtesy of Skinner, Boston and Marlborough, MA

10. *American pilgrim chests*
    Hero and Best photos courtesy of Northeast Auctions, Portsmouth, NH
    Good and Better photos © Christie's Images Limited

11. *Nineteenth-century American dolls*
    Hero and Good photos courtesy of Cowan's Auction, Inc., Cincinnati, OH
    Better photo courtesy of James D. Julia Auctioneers, Fairfield, MA
    Best photo courtesy of Skinner, Boston and Marlborough, MA

12. *Globes*
    Hero, Good, Better, and Best photos reprinted by permission from *House Beautiful*, Hearst Communications, Inc.

13. *Audubon prints*
    Hero, Good, Better, and Best photos courtesy of Skinner, Boston and Marlborough, MA

14. *Sterling napkin rings*
    Good and Best photos © Leslie Hindman Auctioneers, Inc., Chicago, IL
    Hero and Better photos courtesy of Skinner, Boston and Marlborough, MA

15. *Windsor chairs*
    Hero, Good, Better, and Best photos reprinted by permission from *House Beautiful,* Hearst Communications, Inc.

16. *Twentieth-century American hand-painted porcelain*
    Better photo courtesy of Cowan's Auction, Inc., Cincinnati, OH
    Hero photo courtesy of Skinner, Boston and Marlborough, MA
    Good and Best photos by Brad Hobart and courtesy of DuMouchelles Art Gallery, Detroit, MI

17. *Nakashima coffee tables*
    Hero, Good, Better, and Best photos courtesy of Rago Arts and Auction Center, Lambertville, NJ

18. *Cocktail shakers*
    Hero, Good, Better, and Best photos reprinted by permission from *House Beautiful,* Hearst Communications, Inc.

19. *Silhouettes*
    Hero, Good, Better, and Best photos reprinted by permission from *House Beautiful,* Hearst Communications, Inc.

20. *Blue glass*
    Hero and Good photos courtesy of Skinner, Boston and Marlborough, MA
    Better photo courtesy of Brunk Auctions, Asheville, NC
    Best photo courtesy of Sotheby's London

21. *Eighteenth-century English porcelain figures*
    Hero, Good, Better, and Best photos courtesy of Sotheby's

22. *English tea tables*
    Hero and Good photos courtesy of Brunk Auctions, Asheville, NC
    Better photo courtesy of Skinner, Boston and Marlborough, MA
    Best photo courtesy of Sotheby's London

23. *Rose medallion punch bowls*
    Hero, Good, and Best photos courtesy of Dawson & Nye, Morris Plains, NJ
    Better photo courtesy of James D. Julia Auctioneers, Fairfield, ME

24. *Antique silver plate*
    Hero photo courtesy of Samuel T. Freeman & Co., Philadelphia, PA
    Good photo courtesy of Thomaston Place Auction Galleries, Thomaston, ME

Better photo courtesy of Skinner, Boston and Marlborough, MA
Best photo courtesy of Sotheby's London

25. *Teddy bears*
    Hero, Good, and Best photos © Christie's Images Limited
    Better photo courtesy of Pook & Pook, Inc., Downingtown, PA

26. *American longcase clocks*
    Hero and Best photos courtesy of Northeast Auctions, Portsmouth, NH
    Good photo courtesy of Brunk Auctions, Asheville, NC
    Better photo courtesy of Neal Auction Co., New Orleans, LA

27. *Art Deco jewelry*
    Hero and Best photos © Christie's Images Limited
    Good and Better photos courtesy of Skinner, Boston and Marlborough, MA

28. *Nineteenth-century English porcelain figures*
    Hero and Good photos courtesy of Skinner, Boston and Marlborough, MA
    Better photo courtesy of Samuel T. Freeman & Co., Philadelphia, PA
    Best photo courtesy of Sotheby's

29. *Garden seats*
    Hero, Good, and Better photos courtesy of Skinner, Boston and Marlborough, MA
    Best photo courtesy of Doyle, New York

30. *American classical card tables*
    Hero photo courtesy of James D. Julia Auctioneers, Fairfield, ME
    Good photo courtesy of Pook & Pook, Inc., Downingtown, PA
    Better and Best photos courtesy of Northeast Auctions, Portsmouth, NH

31. *Blankets*
    Hero, Good, Better, and Best photos reprinted by permission from *House Beautiful,* Hearst Communications, Inc.

32. *Nineteenth- and twentieth-century European dolls*
    Hero photo courtesy of Skinner, Boston and Marlborough, MA
    Good and detail photo by Brad Hobart and courtesy of DuMouchelles Art Gallery, Detroit, MI
    Better photo courtesy of Sanford Alderfer Auction Co., Hatfield, PA
    Best photo courtesy of James D. Julia Auctioneers, Fairfield, ME

33. *Candlesticks*
Hero, Good, Better, and Best photos reprinted by
permission from *House Beautiful,* Hearst
Communications, Inc.

34. *Klismos chairs*
Hero photo courtesy of Rago Arts and Auction Center,
Lambertville, NJ
Good photo courtesy of Sloans & Kenyon,
Chevy Chase, MD
Better photo reprinted by permission from *House
Beautiful,* Hearst Communications, Inc.
Best photo courtesy of Sotheby's

35. *Dollhouses*
Hero, Good, Better, and Best photos reprinted by
permission from *House Beautiful,* Hearst
Communications, Inc.

36. *American plates*
Good photo courtesy of Cowan's Auction, Inc.,
Cincinnati, OH
Hero photo © www.EarlyAmerican.com, Rancho Santa
Fe, CA
Better photo courtesy of Samuel T. Freeman & Co.,
Philadelphia, PA
Best photo courtesy of Sotheby's

37. *Clear glass compotes*
Hero and Best photos courtesy of Brunk Auctions,
Asheville, NC
Good photo by Brad Hobart and courtesy of
DuMouchelles Art Gallery, Detroit, MI
Better photo courtesy of Samuel T. Freeman,
Philadelphia, PA

38. *Midcentury coffee tables*
Hero, Good, Better, and Best photos courtesy of Wright,
Chicago, IL

39. *Figural napkin holders*
Hero photo courtesy of Skinner, Boston and
Marlborough, MA
Good photo courtesy of Sloans & Kenyon Auctioneers
and Appraisers, Chevy Chase, MD
Better photo courtesy of Dan Ripley's Antique Helper,
Indianapolis, IN
Best photo courtesy of Sanford Alderfer Auction Co.,
Hatfield, PA

40. *Twentieth-century American Shirley Temple dolls*
Hero photo courtesy of Skinner, Boston and
Marlborough, MA
Good and Better photos courtesy of Sanford Alderfer
Auction Co., Hatfield, PA

Best photo courtesy of James D. Julia
Auctioneers, Fairfield, ME

41. *American shelf clocks*
Hero, Good, and Better photos by Brad Hobart and
courtesy of DuMouchelles Art Gallery, Detroit, MI
Best photo courtesy of Pook & Pook, Inc.,
Downingtown, PA

42. *Chinese Chippendale*
Hero, Better, and Best photos courtesy of Sotheby's
Good photo courtesy of Skinner, Boston and
Marlborough, MA

43. *Aluminum*
Hero, Good, Better, and Best photos reprinted by
permission from *House Beautiful,* Hearst
Communications, Inc.

44. *Dog paintings*
Hero, Better, and Best photos © Christie's Images
Limited
Good photo courtesy of Pook & Pook, Inc.,
Downingtown, PA

45. *Nineteenth-century continental porcelain*
Hero and Better photos courtesy of Samuel T. Freeman
& Co., Philadelphia, PA
Good and Best photos courtesy of Skinner, Boston and
Marlborough, MA

46. *Decorative longcase clocks*
Hero and Better photos © Christie's Images
Limited
Good photo courtesy of Weschler's Auctioneers and
Appraisers, Washington, D.C.
Best photo courtesy of the Doris Duke Charitable
Foundation Archives, Duke Farms, Hillsborough, NJ

47. *Suzanis*
Hero photo reprinted by permission from *House
Beautiful,* Hearst Communications, Inc.
Good and Better photos courtesy of Skinner, Boston and
Marlborough, MA
Best photo courtesy of Sotheby's

48. *Art glass compotes*
Hero photo courtesy of Dan Ripley's Antique Helper
Auctions, Indianapolis, IN
Good and Better photos courtesy of James D. Julia
Auctioneers, Fairfield, ME
Best photo by Brad Hobart and courtesy of
DuMouchelles Art Gallery, Detroit, MI

49. *English Regency card tables*
Hero, Good, Better, and Best photos © Christie's Images Limited

50. *Midcentury lamps*
Hero, Good, Better, and Best photos courtesy of Wright, Chicago, IL

51. *Pilgrim chairs*
Hero photo courtesy of Northeast Auctions, Portsmouth, NH
Good photo courtesy of Pook & Pook, Inc., Downingtown, PA
Better photo courtesy of Skinner, Boston and Marlborough, MA
Best photo courtesy of Sotheby's

52. *Twentieth-century American porcelain*
Hero photo courtesy of Skinner, Boston and Marlborough, MA
Good photo courtesy of Sloans & Kenyon Auctioneers and Appraisers, Chevy Chase, MD
Better and Best photos courtesy of Rago Arts and Auction Center, Lambertville, NJ

53. *Toast racks*
Hero photo courtesy of Samuel T. Freeman & Co., Philadelphia, PA
Good and Better photos courtesy of Rago Arts and Auction Center, Lambertville, NJ
Best photo courtesy of Sotheby's London

54. *Cameo glass*
Hero photo courtesy of Sotheby's
Good and Better photos courtesy of Skinner, Boston and Marlborough, MA
Best photo courtesy of Northeast Auctions, Portsmouth, NH

55. *Twentieth-century silver plate*
Hero photo courtesy of Pook & Pook, Inc., Downington, PA
Good and Better photos courtesy of Brunk Auctions, Asheville, NC
Best photo © Christie's Images Limited

56. *Eighteenth-century European dolls*
Hero and Better photos courtesy of Skinner, Boston and Marlborough, MA
Good photo courtesy of Noel Barrett, Carversville, PA
Best photo © Christie's Images Limited

57. *Continental empire tables*
Hero, Good, Better, and Best photos © Christie's Images Limited

58. *Teapots*
Hero, Good, Better, and Best photos reprinted by permission from *House Beautiful,* Hearst Communications, Inc.

59. *Weather Vanes*
Hero photo courtesy of Rago Arts and Auction Center, Lambertville, NJ
Good photo courtesy of Pook & Pook, Inc., Downingtown, PA
Better photo courtesy of Brunk Auctions, Asheville, NC
Best photo courtesy of Sotheby's

60. *Four-poster beds*
Hero photo courtesy of Brunk Auctions, Asheville, NC
Good and Better photos courtesy of Sloans & Kenyon Auctioneers and Appraisers, Chevy Chase, MD
Best photo courtesy of Rago Arts and Auction Center, Lambertville, NJ

61. *Sunburst mirrors*
Hero, Good, Better, and Best photos reprinted by permission from *House Beautiful,* Hearst Communications, Inc.

62. *Midcentury dining tables*
Hero, Good, and Better photos courtesy of Rago Arts and Auction Center, Lambertville, NJ
Best photo courtesy of Wright, Chicago, IL

63. *Travel posters*
Hero, Good, Better, and Best photos reprinted by permission from *House Beautiful,* Hearst Communications, Inc.

64. *Eighteenth-century continental porcelain figures*
Hero and Better photos courtesy of Samuel T. Freeman & Co., Philadelphia, PA
Good and Best photos courtesy of Skinner, Boston and Marlborough, MA

65. *Wineglasses*
Hero and Best photos courtesy of Skinner, Boston and Marlborough, MA
Good photo by Brad Hobart and courtesy of DuMouchelles Art Gallery, Detroit, MI
Better photo courtesy of James D. Julia Auctioneers, Fairfield, ME

Index

Page numbers *in italics* refer to illustrations.